Implementing International Watercourses Law through the WEF Nexus and SDGs

International Water Law

Volumes published in this Brill Research Perspective are listed at *brill.com/rpwl*

Implementing International Watercourses Law through the WEF Nexus and SDGs

An Integrated Approach Illustrated in the Zambezi River Basin

By

Zeray Yihdego
Julie Gibson

BRILL

LEIDEN | BOSTON

This paperback book edition is simultaneously published as issue 5.3 of *International Water Law*, DOI: 10.1163/23529369-12340019.

Library of Congress Control Number: 2020945556

Typeface for the Latin, Greek, and Cyrillic scripts: "Brill". See and download: brill.com/brill-typeface.

ISBN 978-90-04-44470-6 (paperback)
ISBN 978-90-04-44471-3 (e-book)

This book is printed on acid-free paper and produced in a sustainable manner.

Contents

To the memory of Judge Jens Ingebret Evensen (1917–2004), in recognition of his valuable contribution to the development of international water law through his work as one of the International Law Commission rapporteurs to the UN Watercourses Convention, as an International Court of Justice judge, and as a minister in the Norwegian government.

Implementing International Watercourses Law through the WEF Nexus and SDGs: an Integrated Approach Illustrated in the Zambezi River Basin

Zeray Yihdego
Professor and Chair of Public International Law, School of Law, University of Aberdeen, United Kingdom
zeray.yihdego@abdn.ac.uk

Julie Gibson
Doctoral Researcher, Strathclyde Centre for Environmental Law and Governance, Strathclyde School of Law, United Kingdom
julie.gibson@abdn.ac.uk

Abstract

International watercourses law, as primarily codified in the UN Watercourses Convention which reflects the basic principles of customary international water law, provides only a broad framework for states to follow. It does not explicitly address the trade-offs of water uses across multiple sectors, such as energy and food, and the interplay between water and sustainable development. These gaps could be filled by turning to policy frameworks such as the Water-Energy-Food Nexus (WEF) and the global development agendas, such as the Sustainable Development Goals (SDGs). This monograph argues that utilizing these frameworks in an integrated manner could aid riparian states and non-state actors in the consideration of competing water uses, thereby helping to resolve tensions and promoting cooperation among concerned states, as demonstrated using the Zambezi River Basin as a case study.

Keywords

international watercourses law – Sustainable Development Goals – water governance – Water-Energy-Food Nexus – Zambezi basin

 | DOI:10.1163/9789004444713_002

1 Introduction

The governance of international watercourses has to overcome diverse social, economic, religious and ethnic differences traversing across international borders. At the same time, a balance must be struck between complex trade-offs and needs while protecting the longevity of the watercourse and its ecosystem. Cooperation is therefore essential in the management of such watercourses, often guided by the principles of international watercourses law (IWL). Yet, in many ways, IWL provides only a broad framework for states to follow and is not sufficient to systematically consider the trade-offs of water use across multiple sectors such as energy and food. This gap could potentially be filled by turning to policy frameworks, such as the Water-Energy-Food (WEF) nexus, and global development agendas, such as the Sustainable Development Goals (SDGS),[1] which could add further substance to the broad provisions contained in IWL.

Utilizing these three frameworks in an integrated manner, termed the Law, Nexus, Goals (LNG) approach, could aid riparian states and non-state actors in the consideration of competing water uses, thereby helping to resolve tensions and promote cooperation between concerned states and their communities. This approach has been applied to the Zambezi River Basin (ZRB), an extremely complex and fast-developing watercourse with a strong history of cooperation. Our findings demonstrate that even where sound IWL frameworks and cooperative processes exist, this does not guarantee a focused, measurable and sustainable outcome that is capable of addressing tensions among riparians and competing water uses in all cases. A more integrated and holistic framework could go some way to developing a comprehensive and progressive water governance approach within transboundary river basins. Although this integrated approach is not without some drawbacks, such as the continued proliferation of frameworks and paradigms within the sector of water governance, it is argued that the LNG approach offers the potential to build on understanding and further implementation of key principles of IWL. In light of this the key features of the monograph will be introduced in the following sections.

1 United Nations General Assembly (UNGA), '*Transforming Our World: The 2030 Agenda for Sustainable Development*', 21 October 2015, UNGA Resolution 70/1, UN Doc. A/RES/70/1 [SDGS].

International watercourses[2] are vital resources for all forms of life. For humanity they provide, *inter alia*, access to essential water and sanitation services, opportunities for hydropower development, the water supply for small, medium and mega irrigation, and are often a hotspot for tourism activities. The same resources support more than 100,000 species,[3] from fish to large mammals, and are responsible for the maintenance of vital freshwater ecosystems.[4] These shared watercourses are critical resources for the socio-economic growth and advancement of both developed and developing countries alike. Today, consideration of the interdependencies between these water uses have never been more crucial given the increasing pressures placed on water resources as a result of global changes such as population growth, climate change, and the increased use of renewable energy resources.[5]

Furthermore, at the time of writing this monograph, the world is fighting to control the Coronavirus pandemic, resulting from the disease termed COVID-19 that is taking hundreds of thousands of lives and has infected over 25 million people worldwide (as of August 2020); sanitation in general and washing hands in particular have become crucial to containing the spread of

2 The exact terminology of freshwater bodies and what they constitute hydrologically, including their hydrological boundaries, differs both within hydrological disciplinary perspectives and legal interpretations. This monograph uses the term 'international watercourse' in line with the legal definition found in the Convention on the Law of the Non-Navigational Uses of International Watercourses (adopted 21 May 1997, entered into force 17 August 2014), UN Doc A/51/869 [UNWC] for consistency. Article 2(b) states that an international watercourse 'means a watercourse, parts of which are situated in different States', the meaning of 'watercourse' is defined within Article 2(a) as 'a system of surface waters and groundwaters constituting by virtue of their physical relationship a unitary whole and normally flowing into a common terminus'. It should also be noted that Article 2 is only concerned with the non-navigational uses of international watercourses, as navigational and non-navigational uses are treated differently within international law. However, it should also be noted that Article 1(2) of the UNWC provides that where navigational uses impact other water uses, such as water quality, they fall under the substantive norms of the Convention. For further analysis see A. Rieu-Clarke, '*Definition and Use of Terms*', in L. Boisson de Chazournes, M. M. Mbengue, M. Tignino et al., (eds), *The UN Convention on the Law of the Non-Navigational Uses of International Watercourses : A Commentary* (1st ed., Oxford: OUP, 2018) 45–50.

3 World Wildlife Fund (WWF), 'Freshwater Habitat Overview', https://www.worldwildlife.org/habitats/freshwaters, accessed 25 February 2020.

4 R. Moynihan, '*Inland Water Biodiversity: International Law on Protection of Transboundary Freshwater Ecosystems and Biodiversity*', in M. G. Faure (Ed.), *Elgar Encyclopedia of Environmental Law* (Cheltenham: Edward Elgar, 2016) 189–202.

5 See S. C. McCaffrey, C. Leb & R. T. Denoon, 'Introduction to the Research Handbook on International Water Law', in S. C. McCaffrey, C. Leb & R. T. Denoon (Eds.), *Research Handbook on International Water Law* (Cheltenham: Edward Elgar, 2019) 1–9.

the virus and saving lives. However, several countries are experiencing a shortage of (clean) water to comply with World Health Organization guidelines and recommendations to fight the disease as 'more than 40% of the world's population lack adequate access to basic handwashing facilities … Most of these reside in Asia and Africa'.[6] Given that shared watercourses cover up to 40% of human water needs, their governance, protection, and availability are vital in terms of fighting diseases such as COVID-19.

By nature, international watercourses do not belong to a single political or geographical boundary, which makes them subject to multiple governance frameworks with control dispersed across riparian states. The approach taken by each state is often defined by the economic and political priorities of each country, in addition to the physical, geographical and hydrological characteristics of each part of the watercourse. This results in a complex web of different legal and institutional frameworks which aim to respond to a variety of problems. In response, the legal regime of IWL has emerged,[7] now largely recognized in customary international law and contained within two global instruments: the United Nations Watercourses Convention (UNWC)[8] and the United Nations Economic Commission for Europe Convention on the Protection and Use of Transboundary Watercourses and International Lakes (UNECE Water Convention).[9] Together, these two global conventions provide a normative framework built on a number of key principles, as will be described in Section 2.1 below. Yet, IWL alone is not always able to fully identify all of the issues at play or find appropriate solutions to complex problems. As a result, a number of water resource management paradigms have emerged in an attempt to balance competing uses and trade-offs, such as integrated water

6 K. Matheswaran, 'Access to water and COVID-19: Seven measures countries in Asia can take now', Perspectives [blog], Stockholm Environment Institute, 2 April 2020, https://www.sei.org/perspectives/access-to-clean-water-is-vital-in-the-fight-against-covid-19-here-are-seven-measures-that-countries-in-asia-can-take-now/, accessed 10 April 2020.

7 While it can be said that the regime of IWL has been 'emerging' for many years prior to the UNWC and United Nations Economic Commission for Europe (UNECE) Convention on the Protection and Use of Transboundary Watercourses and International Lakes [UNECE Water Convention], this monograph will focus mainly on the key principles that have been codified within the two global instruments. For the historical development of IWL, see S. C. McCaffrey, '*The Path to the UN Watercourses Convention and Beyond*' in Boisson de Chazournes et al., *supra* note 2, 1–18.

8 UNWC, *supra* note 2.

9 Adopted 17 March 1992, 1936 UNTS 269, as amended.

resource management (IWRM),[10] water security,[11] nature-based solutions[12] and the water-energy-food (WEF) nexus,[13] the last of which will be the focus of this monograph.[14] While such frameworks are undoubtedly useful, with each approaching water governance from a new angle, the extent to which each of these paradigms is truly novel and able to ignite change can be debated.[15] Focus should not be placed on attempts to 'reinvent the wheel', but rather to look holistically at the governance frameworks that currently exist and work towards integration that looks beyond the water sector and adds more substance to key IWL provisions.

The WEF nexus hinges on two of the main water uses and sources of conflict (energy and food production) and is particularly essential for consideration within the context of developing countries due to the rate at which

10 The Global Water Partnership (GWP) defines IWRM as 'a process which promotes the coordinated development and management of water, land and related resources in order to maximise economic and social welfare in an equitable manner without compromising the sustainability of vital ecosystems and the environment'. GWP, 'About IWRM' (2018), https://www.gwp.org/en/gwp-SAS/ABOUT-GWP-SAS/WHY/About-IWRM/, accessed 24 July 2020. For a legal perspective of IWRM, see A. Allan & A. Rieu-Clarke, '*Good Governance and IWRM: A Legal Perspective*', 24, Irrigation and Drainage Systems (2010) 239–248.

11 Water security is defined by the United Nations as '[t]he capacity of a population to safeguard sustainable access to adequate quantities of and acceptable quality water for sustaining livelihoods, human well-being, and socio-economic development, for ensuring protection against water-borne pollution and water-related disasters, and for preserving ecosystems in a climate of peace and political stability'. See UN-Water, *Water Security & The Global Water Agenda: An Analytical Brief* (Hamilton, ON: United Nations University, 2013), https://collections.unu.edu/eserv/UNU:2651/Water-Security-and-the-Global-Water-Agenda.pdf, accessed 12 June 2019.

12 Nature-based solutions are defined by the International Union for Conservation of Nature (IUCN) as 'actions to protect, sustainably manage, and restore natural or modified ecosystems, that address societal challenges effectively and adaptively, simultaneously providing human well-being and biodiversity benefits'. See IUCN, Commission on Ecosystem Management, 'Nature-based Solutions', https://www.iucn.org/commissions/commission-ecosystem-management/our-work/nature-based-solutions, accessed 12 June 2019.

13 Definitions of the water-energy-food (WEF) nexus vary, however, most agree on core aspects, including complex interdependencies and linkages between each of the water, energy and food sectors, which includes potential trade-offs and feedback between each sector. Further details will be provided in Section 2.2 of this monograph.

14 R. Schweizer & C. Bréthaut, '*From the Promises of International Water Management Trends to the Reality of Policies and Practices: Some Conclusive Thoughts*', in C. Bréthaut & R. Schweizer (Eds.), *A Critical Approach to International Water Management Trends: Policy and Practice* (London: Palgrave Macmillan, 2018) 269–293.

15 *Id.*

development is occurring in these sectors.[16]As stated by Pahl-Wostl, 'interdependencies between these resources have often been neglected in sectoral policies with the consequence of persistent trade-offs rather than identification and strengthening of synergies'.[17] Integration with other sectors is not new in the world of water governance; it has been advocated since the emergence of IWRM, which has been widely incorporated into national and international policies relating to the governance of water resources.[18] IWRM emerged as a dominant paradigm for the management of water resources in the early 1990s, and was frequently linked to Agenda 21[19] and calls for holistic management of water resources.[20] IWRM appreciates the cross-sectoral relevance of water which requires integration with other natural resource management processes, including land and ecosystems.[21] Its rejection of fragmented and singular approaches resonates with the WEF nexus, however, IWRM places less emphasis on the role of water in the production of food or its use in energy. IWRM has also been fraught with difficulties in implementation, largely driven by a lack of institutional capacity to govern across different sectoral borders, such as energy and agriculture. This institutional difficulty is also faced by a WEF nexus approach.[22] In order to deal with the lack of integration between institutions, this monograph proposes combining the WEF nexus with the SDGs, an agenda which already has global political commitment and can infer

16 An example of such conflict can be seen in the Blue Nile Dam controversy; Ethiopia wants to generate electricity while Egypt (and Sudan) need water for agriculture. See Z. Yihdego & A. Rieu-Clarke, '*An Exploration of Fairness in International Law through the Blue Nile and GERD*', 41:4, Water International (2016) 528–549.

17 C. Pahl-Wostl, '*Governance of the Water-Energy-Food Security Nexus: A Multi-Level Coordination Challenge*', 92, Environmental Science & Policy (2019) 356–367.

18 For further details on the use of IWRM globally, see M. Bertule, P. Glennie, P.K. Bjørnsen et al., '*Monitoring Water Resources Governance Progress Globally: Experiences from Monitoring SDG Indicator 6.5.1 on Integrated Water Resources Management Implementation*', 10:12, Water (Switzerland) (2018) 1744.

19 Agenda 21 is a non-binding plan of action to be taken globally, nationally and locally with regard to development and the environment. The plan was the main outcome document of the Rio Convention, see United Nations, *Agenda 21: A Programme for Action for Sustainable Development*, UN Doc A/CONF.151/26 (Vol. II) (13 June 1992), Annex II.

20 G. Aguilar & I. Alejandro, *Governance of Shared Waters: Legal and Institutional Issues* (Gland: IUCN, 2011).

21 *Id.*, at 27.

22 For an analysis of the relationship between the WEF Nexus and IWRM, see D. Benson, A.K. Gain & J.J. Rouillard, '*Water Governance in a Comparative Perspective: From IWRM to a 'Nexus' Approach?*', 8, Water Alternatives (2015) 756–773.

normative influence when used by states in the application of IWL, as well as within their own domestic law and policy frameworks.[23]

From the perspective of Otto Spijkers and of this monograph, the SDGs can 'add substantive flesh to the otherwise abstract skeleton of general international water law'.[24] While the expression 'abstract skeleton' must be taken with caution, Spijkers rightly notes that the 'concrete political commitment' of the SDGs can be 'attached' to the norms of IWL, providing cross fertilization. The SDGs will be used within this monograph in the same way; that is, as additional 'substance' for the interpretation and application of the broad provisions contained within IWL, which without such expansion can be viewed as an 'abstract skeleton' at worst and a generally vague legal framework at best.

The SDGs build upon the Millennium Development Goals (MDGs),[25] which formed the first global framework to set specific targets for global development. The SDGs follow the same course, with a new set of 17 goals and 169 targets that are universal in nature. The SDGs are legally non-binding,[26] and as such

---

23 Existing literature on the relationship between IWL, WEF and the SDGs has linked two of the three frameworks, but no literature considers all three. For discussion of the relationship between the WEF nexus and the SDGs, see J. Terrapon-Pfaff, W. Ortiz, C. Dienst & M-C. Gröne, '*Energising the WEF Nexus to Enhance Sustainable Development at Local Level*', 223, Journal of Environmental Management (2018) 409–416; R. M. Stephan, R. H. Mohtar, B. Daher et al., '*Water—Energy—Food Nexus: A Platform for Implementing the Sustainable Development Goals*', 43:3, Water International (2018) 472–479; I. Boas, F. Biermann & N. Kanie, '*Cross-sectoral Strategies in Global Sustainability Governance: Towards a Nexus Approach*', 16, International Environmental Agreements: Politics, Law & Economics (2016) 449–464; M. Fader, C. Cranmer, R. Lawford & J. Engel-Cox, '*Toward an Understanding of Synergies and Trade-Offs Between Water, Energy, and Food SDG Targets*', 6, Frontiers in Environmental Science (2018) 112, DOI:10.3389/fenvs.2018.00112; Pahl-Wostl, *supra* note 17. Some literature has also developed perspectives on the relationship between IWL and the sustainable development goals, namely Goal 6 (the water goal), see A. Belinskij, '*Water-Energy-Food Nexus within the Framework of International Water Law*', 7:10, Water (Switzerland) (2015) 5396–5415; Orme, M., Z. Cuthbert, F. Sindico et al., '*Good Transboundary Water Governance in the 2015 Sustainable Development Goals: A Legal Perspective*', 40:7, Water International (2015) 969–983 Benson, Gain & Rouillard, *supra* note 22.

24 O. Spijkers, '*The Cross-fertilization between the Sustainable Development Goals and International Water Law*', 25:1, Review of European Comparative & International Environmental Law (2016) 39–49.

25 UN General Assembly, '*United Nations Millennium Declaration*', 18 September 2000, UNGA Resolution 55/2, UN Doc A/RES/55/2. It must be noted that while the SDGs are universal in nature, the MDGs applied only to developing countries.

26 For discussion on the notion of sustainable development, see V. Lowe, '*Sustainable Development and Unsustainable Arguments*', in A. Boyle & D. Freestone (Eds.), *International Law and Sustainable Development: Past Achievements and Future Challenges* (Oxford: OUP, 1999) 19–37, 23.

their achievement will need to be supported by formal rules of domestic and international law.[27] However, despite not directly providing a legal obligation by nature, the SDGs demonstrate strong political commitment that can be utilized towards the implementation of an LNG approach.[28] This monograph will focus mainly on the three sectoral goals linked to the WEF nexus but will also give due reference to other key goals such as mitigating climate change and cooperation at the international level.

To provide further understanding of the LNG approach a case study of the ZRB will form the substance of Section 3 of this monograph. Expansion of hydropower dams, irrigation schemes and population growth are only three of the many complex developments taking place within the ZRB. The ZRB has a strong history of cooperation between its riparian states; although management measures for the watercourse have, both historically and to date, struggled to balance the preservation of the Zambezi River basin with the regions need for economic growth and development, particularly in the area of hydropower.[29] This context makes the ZRB an appropriate case study for the implementation of new methodologies such as the integrated IWL, the

27 In this sense, the SDGs, like the MDGs before them, demonstrate a new trend in international environmental law whereby progress is made in the form of political commitments as opposed to legally binding norms. However, several of the goals are directly relevant to international human rights law, socio-economic and cultural rights in particular. See International Covenant on Economic, Social and Cultural Rights (ICESCR) 1966. Article 11 of the Covenant recognizes 'the right of everyone to an adequate standard of living', which must be read in conjunction with Article 2 (1) which obliges states to take steps 'to the maximum of its available resources, with a view to achieving progressively the full realization of the rights recognized'. Further, the human right to water was recognized in November 2002 through General Comment No. 15 which defined the right to water as the right to 'sufficient, safe, acceptable, physically accessible and affordable water for personal and domestic uses'. In 2010 the human right to water was formally recognized by the UN General Assembly through Resolution 64/292 and further affirmed through Resolution 15/9, which recognized the right to water as part of existing international law and confirms the right to be binding upon states. UN Committee on Economic, Social and Cultural Rights, '*General Comment No.15: The Right to Water (Arts. 11 and 12 of the Covenant)*', UN Doc. E/C.12/2002/11 (20 January 2003) UN General Assembly, '*The Human Right to Water and Sanitation*', 28 July 2010, UNGA Resolution 64/292, UN Doc. A/RES/64/292; Human Rights Council, 'Human rights and access to safe drinking water and sanitation', UN Doc A/HRC/Res/15/9 (6 October 2010).

28 For discussion on the 'soft law' nature of the SDGs see M. M. T. Brus, '*Soft Law in Public International Law: A Pragmatic or Principled Choice? Comparing the Sustainable Development Goals and the Paris Agreement*', in P. Westerman, J. Hage, S. Kirste & A. R. Mackor, (eds), *Legal Validity and Soft Law* (Cham: Springer, 2107), 243–266, https://papers.ssrn.com/sol3/papers.cfm?abstract_id=2945942, accessed 11 May 2020.

29 See A. Tilmant, A., W. Kinzelbach, D. Juizo et al., '*Economic Valuation of Benefits and Costs Associated with the Coordinated Development and Management of the Zambezi River Basin*', 14, Water Policy (2012) 490–508.

WEF nexus and SDG approach proposed in this monograph, which could be successfully implemented as a result of the existing cooperative frameworks already in place.

The key question this monograph explores is the extent to which an LNG approach can aid and reinforce the implementation of the core principles of IWL. More specifically, it will demonstrate how the SDGs and WEF nexus can be mutually supportive in tackling the tension between competing uses and trade-offs between sectors without undermining the law. It will illustrate how this approach can, as a result, assist states with fulfilling their international legal commitments relating to IWL by filling substantive gaps in the law. The framework can develop a common language to negotiate risks of cooperation according to the priorities of countries sharing an international watercourse, encouraging cooperation and negotiation and supporting the integration of fragmented institutional systems. This monograph will therefore contribute to scholarship on international watercourses by proposing a novel approach to the governance of international watercourses through the integration of the three frameworks identified above. A further contribution to literature is made through a comprehensive analysis of the most up-to-date legal and institutional structures of the ZRB.

The monograph is divided into four sections: section 1 provides an overview of the normative and conceptual frameworks that are used, including IWL, the WEF nexus and the SDGs. The purpose of this section is to articulate the features of these frameworks and the gaps therein when applied independently. Section 2 discusses the main argument proposed in the monograph: integrating the WEF nexus and the SDGs to aid implementation of IWL. It illustrates the potential trade-offs and synergies of the frameworks and demonstrates how their integration can allow countries to benefit from a systematic and holistic application of relevant laws, policies and targets while fulfilling their international legal commitments. Section 3 provides the application of this integrated method to the case study of the ZRB. Finally, Section 4 provides concluding remarks and proposed insights.

2 Normative and Conceptual Frameworks

IWL, the WEF nexus and the SDGs are each discussed within a wealth of literature.[30] Therefore, while this section provides an overview of each of the

30 Despite the rich literature which exists on the WEF nexus, there is little discussion of the role of legal frameworks in general and international law specifically. C. Pahl-Wostl, A. Bhaduri & A. Bruns, '*Editorial Special Issue: The Nexus of Water, Energy and Food—An*

frameworks for the purposes of clarity in subsequent sections, it does not repeat in-depth analysis of each framework itself, which can be found in work produced by others. This section begins with an outline of the key principles of IWL, demonstrating their relevance to the issues and problems addressed in the monograph. It then discusses the 'WEF nexus' as a conceptual and analytical tool that can be used to frame an approach to the governance of international watercourses and as a means of addressing the tensions between different uses and sectors. Finally, it discusses the SDGs and their relevance to both IWL and the WEF. Overall, it provides an introduction to each of the core elements of an LNG approach to water governance.

2.1 *International Water Law*

The intention here is not to analyse the corpus of IWL, but rather to provide a novel approach to its implementation through the utilization of the WEF nexus and the SDGs.[31] The focus of discussion is predominately on the UNWC although it is recognized that there are many other multilateral and bilateral water treaties, as well as a number of regional and basin level frameworks, to which reference will be given where applicable.[32] The UNECE Water Convention will also be discussed intermittently due to its complementary relationship with

Environmental Governance Perspective', 90, Environmental Science & Policy (2018) 161–163; L. Nhamo, B. Ndlela, C. Nhemachena et al., '*The Water-Energy-Food Nexus: Climate Risks and Opportunities in Southern Africa*', 10:5, Water (Switzerland) (2018) 567; Pahl-Wostl, *supra* note 17; Boas et al., *supra* note 23; L. De Strasser, A. Lipponen, M. Howells et al., '*A Methodology to Assess the Water Energy Food Ecosystems Nexus in Transboundary River Basins*', 8:2, Water (Switzerland) (2016) 59; M. Muller, 'The "Nexus" as a Step Back towards a More Coherent Water Resource Management Paradigm', 8:1, Water Alternatives (2015) 675–694; A. Smajgl, J. Ward & L. Pluschke, '*The Water-Food-Energy Nexus—Realising a New Paradigm*', 533, Journal of Hydrology (2016) 533–540; Stephan et al., *supra* note 23; Tilmant et al., *supra* note 29; A. Bhaduri, C. Ringler, I. Dombrowski et al. 'Sustainability in the Water—Energy—Food Nexus', 40, Water International (2105) 723–732.

31 There are many resources which provide through analysis of IWL, particularly the UNWC. Recently published resources include Boisson de Chazournes et al., *supra* note 2; M. Tignino & C. Bréthaut (Eds.), Research Handbook on Freshwater Law and International Relations (Cheltenham: Edward Elgar, 2018); McCaffrey, Leb & Denoon, *supra* note 5.

32 Additional international and regional level legal frameworks which will be covered within the scope of this monograph include the UNECE Watercourses Convention, *supra* note 9; Revised Protocol on Shared Watercourses in the Southern African Development Community (signed 7 August 2000; in force 22 September 2003) [SADC Revised Protocol]; Agreement on the Establishment of the Zambezi Watercourse Commission (ZAMCOM) (signed 13 August 2004, in force 19 June 2011) [ZAMCOM Agreement].

the UNWC and existence at the international level.[33] However, the UNWC more so than the UNECE Water Convention reflects the substantive and procedural norms of customary international law and will therefore be the main instrument discussed.[34]

Two principles form the foundation of IWL: equitable and reasonable utilization and the 'no harm rule'.[35] These two principles, in addition to the general duty to cooperate, act as the substantive core of the UNWC. They are implemented through several procedural provisions contained within the second half of the instrument. Yet, specific mechanisms for operationalization remain sparse and the provisions themselves are vague. While the UNWC clearly details these two basic principles, the UNECE Water Convention goes into greater detail in relation to more 'modern' concepts of IWL such as pollution prevention and environmental protection.[36] Further, the UNECE Water Convention not only requires states to establish joint bodies (Article 9), but also provides for meetings of the parties (Article 17) and a secretariat (Article 19), all of which are absent from the UNWC, but are features of most modern multilateral environmental agreements. Provisions in the UNWC are characterized by a high level of generality in order to apply to widely varying hydrological, climatological and developmental conditions. The UNECE Water Convention on the other hand provides further detail on implementation through its *Guide to Implementing the Water Convention*.[37] Overall focus within the UNWC

33 Considering the mutual supportiveness of the frameworks, Rieu-Clarke and Kinna describe how the UNWC and UNECE Watercourses Convention can be used to provide a 'package approach' to the law of international watercourses. see A. Rieu-Clarke & R. Kinna, '*Can Two Global UN Water Conventions Effectively Co-exist? Making the Case for a 'Package Approach' to Support Institutional Coordination*', 23 1, Review of European, Comparative & International Environmental Law (2014) 15–31.

34 See S. C. McCaffrey, '*The Customary Law of International Watercourses*' in Tignino & Bréthaut, *supra* note 31, 147–174. See also *Gabčíkovo-Nagymaros Project (Hungary v. Slovakia)*, Judgment (Merits), [1997] ICJ Rep 4, p. 7; *Pulp Mills on the River Uruguay (Argentina v. Uruguay)*, Judgment, [2010] ICJ Rep 14, p. 14. The influence of the principles contained in the UNWC can also be clearly demonstrated by their incorporation in regional and basin level frameworks, as will be demonstrated in subsequent sections dealing with Southern Africa.

35 O. McIntyre, '*Substantive Rules of International Water Law*', in A. Rieu-Clarke, A. Allan & S. Hendry (Eds.), *Routledge Handbook of Water Law and Policy* (London and New York: Routledge, 2017) 234–246.

36 See UNECE Water Convention, *supra* note 9, Art. 2.

37 UNECE, *Guide to Implementing the Water Convention* (New York and Geneva: United Nations, 2013), https://www.unece.org/fileadmin/DAM/env/water/publications/WAT_Guide_to_implementing_Convention/ECE_MP.WAT_39_Guide_to_implementing_

is placed on water quantity, while the UNECE Water Convention emphasizes water quality; thus, the two instruments are, in many ways, complementary and mutually reinforcing.[38]

The following sections will consider each of the substantive principles of IWL in turn, followed by a brief overview of the procedural provisions. The principles will not be treated equally as equitable and reasonable use and no significant harm are the main provisions of concern for the purposes of this monograph. Therefore, greater emphasis will be placed on unpacking the meaning and interpretation of these two principles.

2.1.1 Equitable and Reasonable Use

The principle of equitable and reasonable use is found in Articles 5 and 6 of the UNWC. Article 5 sets out the principle itself, while Article 6 provides a non-exhaustive list of 'factors' which should be taken into consideration when determining what is equitable and reasonable. Article 5 notes that watercourse states 'shall' use an international watercourse 'in an equitable and reasonable manner'. It further notes that the watercourse should be 'used and developed by watercourse states with a view to attaining optimal and sustainable utilisation thereof and benefits therefrom'.[39] Article 5(2) highlights that participation in the 'use, development and protection' of an international watercourse should include the duty to cooperate. Article 5 therefore demonstrates not only the need to use and protect watercourses in a manner which is equitable and reasonable, but also links this use to sustainability and benefits that can be derived from the watercourse. This wording is significant, linking to both sustainable development and benefit sharing.[40] Article 5 does not, however, provide any definition of what can be considered to be equitable and reasonable, as such a conclusion is to be derived from taking into consideration the factors contained in Article 6.

The factors provided in Article 6 cover natural characteristics such as hydrological streamflow, social and economic need, population dependency,

water_convention_small_size_ENG.pdf, accessed 10 February 2020. See also A. Tanzi, *The Consolidation of International Water Law: A Comparative Analysis of the UN and UNECE Water Conventions* (Editoriale Scientifica Napoli, 2017), https://ssrn.com/abstract=3080819, accessed 12 February 2020.

38 Rieu-Clarke & Kinna, *supra* note 33.

39 UNWC, *supra* note 2, Art. 5(1).

40 For further information on benefit sharing and transboundary river basins, see D. Grey & C. Sadoff, *'Beyond the River: The Benefits of Cooperation on International Rivers'*, 47, Water Science and Technology (2003) 91–96.

existing and potential uses of the watercourse, as well as the viability of alternatives and the 'conservation, protection, development and economy of use' of the watercourse.[41] Critically, Article 6(3) also states:

> The weight to be given to each factor is to be determined by its importance in comparison with that of other relevant factors. In determining what is reasonable and equitable use, all relevant factors are to be considered together and a conclusion reached on the basis of the whole.

The weight of the factors is somewhat elusive; there is no hierarchical list to be considered and no consensus on where to focus greater weight. The only real guidance regarding prioritization is contained within Article 10(2) which states that in the event of a conflict 'special regard' should be given to 'vital human needs'. As noted by Van der Zaag et al. equitable and reasonable use is, therefore, 'defined in general terms and is thus prone to subjective interpretation'.[42] A result of such vagueness, as explained by Lankford, could be that the principle of equitable and reasonable use and its accompanying factors can be misleading to states.[43] Lankford further notes that current use and population should be given more weight than others, given that the former is illustrative of the economic context of the current use and the latter is linked to the realization of the human right to water.[44] This could, however, be difficult to implement as the two factors may give a contradictory result in relation to a particular watercourse. Furthermore, excessive dependence on population and existing use does not guarantee an equitable share among riparian states. Moving from an anthropocentric perspective, Eckstein et al. rightly acknowledge the need for the 'greening' of international water law, giving greater consideration for environmental needs.[45]

---

41 UNWC, *supra* note 2, Art. 6(1)(f).

42 P. Van Der Zaag, P., I. M. Seyam & H. H. G. Savenije, '*Towards Measurable Criteria for the Equitable Sharing of International Water Resources*', 4:1, Water Policy (2002) 19–32, 20.

43 B. Lankford, '*Does Article 6 (Factors Relevant to Equitable and Reasonable Utilization) in the UN Watercourses Convention Misdirect Riparian Countries?*', 38, Water International (2013) 130–145.

44 *Id.*

45 G. Eckstein, G., R. K. Paisley, S. Burchi et al., *The Greening of Water Law: Managing Freshwater Resources for People and the Environment* (UNEP, 2010). For discussion of the relationship between IWL and ecosystem protection, see A. D. Tarlock, '*Safeguarding International River Ecosystems in Times of Scarcity*', 3, University of Denver Water Law Journal (2000) 231–272; O. McIntyre, '*The Protection of Freshwater Ecosystems Revisited: Towards a Common Understanding of the "Ecosystems Approach" to the Protection of*

This is a sound and potentially consensus-gripping argument, although one might argue that attempts to strengthen environmental protection must still be balanced with developmental needs. Nevertheless, this prioritization of factors among authors demonstrates how widely opinions are likely to diverge between states, given the lack of direction contained in the factors themselves. Thus, the operationalization of Article 6 relies on a deliberative process by each state to establish 'importance' and 'weight'. It must be noted that this gap is intentional in the nature of the UNWC as a framework convention, allowing states of an international watercourse to establish such importance and weight based on the specific character of the watercourse concerned. Yet, in doing so, it also leaves significant room for interpretation and, as stated by Lankford it 'leaves unresolved the level of detail and other mechanisms required to take water allocation to a satisfying or unambiguous conclusion'.[46] The complexity of the application of Article 6 is further stated by Dellapenna:

> In attempting to apply the UN Convention [UNWC], one must always recall that 'equitable' does not mean 'equal'—a confusion that can arise in some non-common law countries where the notion of 'equality' in its common law sense is lacking. 'Equity' means a fair share considering the water needs and the availability to use the water efficiently of the several riparian states.[47]

While this statement is correct, as is the interpretation of the law, the importance of equality among concerned riparians of an international watercourse must not be undermined. In this respect, the Permanent Court of International Justice (PCIJ) in the *River Oder* case asserted that

> [the] community of interest in a navigable river becomes the basis of a common legal right, the essential features of which are the perfect equality of all riparian States in the user of the whole course of the river and

Transboundary Water Resources', 23, Review of European, Comparative and International Environmental Law (2014) 88–95; J. Brunnée & S. Toope, '*Environmental Security and Freshwater Resources: Ecosystem Regime Building*', 91, American Journal of International Law (1997) 26–59.

46 Lankford, *supra* note 43.

47 J. W. Dellapenna, '*The Customary International Law of Transboundary Fresh Waters*', 1, International Journal of Global Environmental Issues (2001) 264–305, 286.

> the exclusion of any preferential privilege of any one riparian State in relation to the others.[48]

However, equality does not necessarily imply dividing water in equal numbers. Dellapenna further states:

> Non-lawyers, particularly engineers and hydrologists, sometimes see in these catalogues of factors a poorly stated equation. By this view, if one simply fills in numerical values for each factor, one could somehow calculate each watercourse state's share of the water without reference to political or other non-quantitative variables … Any attempt to treat the list of relevant factors as an algorithm simply misses the point entirely.[49]

This is an important point and goes to the heart of the matter being discussed in this monograph; the factors under Article 6 cannot be treated as definitive and considered in isolation of all other aspects of governance, they must be used in the context of the watercourse, the prevailing situation of concerned riparians and their populations, and in harmony with other law and policy frameworks to adapt to the context of the watercourse in which they are being applied. While Dellapenna highlights the difficulties in the interpretation of the Article 6 factors by 'non-lawyers', it is essential that the consideration of each factor looks beyond the legal sphere to incorporate matters of, *inter alia*, economics, hydrology and sociology. Section 3 of this monograph will illustrate how the WEF nexus and the SDGs can play such a role by providing scientific and policy considerations that are pertinent for the full assessment of the Article 6 factors. Prior to such discussion, attention must be drawn to the second most important rule of IWL, namely the no significant harm rule.

2.1.2 No Significant Harm

In the UNWC the 'no harm rule' is contained in Article 7, which obliges states to 'take all appropriate measures to prevent the causing of significant harm to other watercourse States'.[50] Article 7(2) further notes that where significant harm does occur states shall 'take all appropriate measures, having due regard

48 *Territorial Jurisdiction of the International Commission of the River Oder*, [1929] Judgement No. 16, P.C.I.J., Series A, No. 23, p. 27. This was later endorsed by the ICJ, see, e.g., *Gabčíkovo-Nagymoros Project (Hungary v. Slovakia)*, *supra* note 34, at 57, para 85.

49 Dellapenna, *supra* note 47.

50 UNWC, *supra* note 2, Art. 7(1).

for the provisions of Articles 5 and 6', in other words, for equitable and reasonable use. Despite the inclusion of equitable and reasonable use within Article 7(2) the lack of clarity around question of subordination between the two principles has given rise to significant controversy.[51] However, as stated by Salman, 'it is now widely believed ... that the obligation not to cause significant harm subordinates the principle of equitable and reasonable utilization'.[52] As also stated by Wouters on the relationship between equitable and reasonable use and no significant harm, '[w]hile the former rule might permit significant harm as a result of an equitable use of the watercourse, the latter would not'.[53] This is compatible with the notion that the no harm duty is not absolute, if it happens the state which causes harm shall compensate for the damages and cooperate with the affected state with the purpose of mitigating or eliminating such harm.

The obligation is limited to the duty not to cause *significant* harm. This threshold is also used within the 2001 International Law Commission (ILC) Draft Articles on Prevention of Transboundary Harm from Hazardous Activities,[54] although neither instrument provides any further indication of the activities which may or may not fall within this defined scope.[55] To elaborate on the no-harm rule, McIntyre has linked its due diligence requirements to equitable and reasonable use, noting that the prohibition on causing significant harm could be reached only by taking into account the factors listed in Article 6.[56] While it may be true that consideration of the factors could mitigate significant harm, such an action is, of course, still limited by the lack of specificity contained within the factors themselves.

The complicated relationship between equitable and reasonable use and no significant harm has resulted in the former often (although not always)

---

51 S. M. A. Salman, '*The Obligation Not to Cause Significant Harm (Article 7)*' in Boisson de Chazournes et al., *supra* note 2, 95.

52 *Id.*, at 96.

53 P. K. Wouters, '*An Assessment of Recent Developments in International Watercourse Law through the Prism of the Substantive Rules Governing Use Allocation (River Basins)*', 36:2, Natural Resources Journal (1996) 417–439, 420.

54 International Law Commission, '*Draft Articles on Prevention of Transboundary Harm from Hazardous Activities, with commentaries*' (11 May 2001), in *Report of the International Law Commission on the Work of its Fifty-third Session 23 April–1 June and 2 July–10 August 2001*, UN Doc A/56/10.

55 Identifying the threshold of significant harm is difficult and must be context based, as discussed by Christina Leb in S. McCaffrey, '*Introductory Remarks: The Last Drop: Practical Tools for Addressing Transboundary Water Crises*', in *Proceedings of the 113th ASIL Annual Meeting* (Cambridge: Cambridge University Press, 2019) 313–329, at 324.

56 O. McIntyre, *Environmental Protection of International Watercourses under International Law* (Aldershot: Ashgate Publishing, 2007).

being favoured by upstream states, while the notion of no significant harm has frequently been favoured by downstream states.[57] This preference can also be linked to an assumption which is often made, as stated by Salman, that 'harm can only be caused by upstream riparian's to downstream, because harm can only 'travel' downstream with the flow of the waters'.[58] However, while the causes of harm flowing downstream may be more obvious, such as pollution or reduced water flow, harm can also be caused by states which are downstream by the potential foreclosure of their future use of water.[59] Indeed, the concept of foreclosure has even been included in some basin-wide legal frameworks, such as the Senegal River Water Charter.[60] The language used within the UNWC clearly covers both upstream and downstream states, as no specifications are made.[61] It can also be argued that mismanagement of water resources downstream can affect the entire ecosystem of an international watercourse due to the connectivity of the water system and the environment around river basins, once again demonstrating the need to ensure that the interpretation and subsequent implementation of IWL is based on both legal considerations and scientific evidence.

Reference to harm is also made in a number of other articles throughout the UNWC. Article 12 dictates that the requirement for notification of planned measures only requires such notification when there is 'significant adverse effect'. Article 21, which covers the control of pollution, requires states to 'prevent, reduce, and control' pollution of an international watercourse which may cause 'significant harm'. As noted by Salman, entirely new language relating to harm is subsequently used within Article 22, which covers the introduction of new or alien species, where 'effects detrimental' to the watercourse must be prevented.[62] Once more, there is no further expansion as to the meaning of each of these levels of 'harm' or what the threshold may be for a state to be deemed to have caused such harm. What is clear is that harm comprises both quantitative and qualitative issues such as significant water flow reduction and affecting water quality, respectively.[63]

57 S. M. A. Salman, '*The United Nations Watercourses Convention Ten Years Later: Why Has Its Entry into Force Proven Difficult?*', 32:1, Water International (2007) 1–15.

58 Salman, '*The Obligation Not to Cause Significant Harm (Article 7)*', *supra* note 51, at 115.

59 *Id.*, at 116.

60 Charter of Waters of Senegal River (Charte des Eaux du Fleuve Sénégal) (signed 28 May 2002).

61 Some authors have also linked the two principles with the level of economic development within each state, see K. Wegerich & O. Olsson, '*Late Developers and the Inequity of "Equitable Utilization" and the Harm of "Do No Harm"*', 35:6, Water International (2010) 707–717.

62 Salman, *supra* note 51, '*The Obligation Not to Cause Significant Harm (Article 7)*', at 120.

63 *Id.*, at 121.

The 'no harm' principle has been widely expressed in the case law of the ICJ. In the *Pulp Mills* case, the ICJ articulated the customary rule that '[a] State is ... obliged to use all the means at its disposal in order to avoid activities which take place in its territory, or in any area under its jurisdiction, causing significant damage to the environment of another State'.[64] The *Pulp Mills* ruling followed from earlier cases that expanded and clarified the customary status of the no significant harm principles. The *Trail Smelter Arbitration*[65] noted that 'no State has the right to use or permit the use of its territory in such a manner as to cause injury ... to the territory of another'.[66] In the *Corfu Channel* case, although primarily about issues such as innocent passage and state responsibility for damages, the ICJ offers general guidance relevant to harm, by stating that every country is 'under an obligation not to allow knowingly its territory to be used for acts contrary to the rights of other States'.[67] This statement is similar to that expressed in *Trail Smelter* and illustrates that the Court has not relied on treaty law, but refers to 'certain general and well-recognized principles'.[68] Thus, the ICJ clearly recognized the existence of a general principle of law requiring states to prevent or prohibit harm to other states. It is important to note that the *Corfu Channel* case also makes it clear that it is not only an act which can be seen to cause harm, but also an omission.[69] Subsequently, the nature of the norm has continued to evolve; while the formulation expressed in *Trail Smelter* was used in the formulation of Principle 21 of the 1972 Stockholm Declaration,[70] by 1992 it had advanced further within Principle 2 of the Rio Declaration.[71] Principle 21 noted that states have 'the sovereign right to exploit their resources' pursuant to their own environmental policies and the 'responsibility to ensure that activities within their jurisdiction or control do not cause damage' to the environment of other States'.[72] In

64 *Pulp Mills on the River Uruguay* (*Argentina v. Uruguay*), Judgment, [2010] ICJ Rep 14, at 56, para 101.

65 *Trail Smelter Arbitration* (*United States v. Canada*), 3 R.I.A.A. 1911 [1938, 1941].

66 *Id.*, at 1965.

67 *Corfu Channel Case* (*United Kingdom/Albania*), Judgment (Merits), [1949] ICJ Rep 4, at 22.

68 *Id.*

69 *Id.*, at 23.

70 United Nations, '*Declaration of the United Nations Conference on the Human Environment*', in *Report of the United Nations Conference on the Human Environment, Stockholm, 5–16 June 1972*, UN Doc A/CONF.48/14/REV.1 (New York: United Nations, 1973) [Stockholm Declaration].

71 United Nations General Assembly, '*Rio Declaration on Environment and Development, Rio de Janeiro, 13 June 1992*', in *Report of the United Nations Conference on Environment and Development*, UN Doc. A/CONF.151/26 (12 August 1992), Annex 1 [Rio Declaration].

72 Stockholm Declaration, *supra* note 70, Principle 21.

Principle 2 of the Rio Declaration the wording was altered to 'their own environmental and developmental policies' thereby recognizing the importance of striking a balance between environmental and developmental goals.[73]

This leaves us with three takeaways with respect to the duty of significant harm: first, it is one of the most important but controversial rules of IWL; secondly, the duty is imposed on all riparian states of an international watercourse; and thirdly, it subordinates the core principle, equitable and reasonable use and other issues such as concerns of pollution. As is the case with equitable and reasonable use, determining what can be considered as 'significant harm' is difficult and must be dealt with on a case-by-case basis by concerned parties, appropriate commissions, panels of experts or courts and tribunals based upon available evidence.[74] The definition of such harm can be expanded on by each country through a consideration of factors which run much wider than water quality or quantity, as will be demonstrated in Section 3 with regard to the WEF nexus and the SDGs. While the rules of equitable and reasonable use and no significant harm are vital principles for the governance of international watercourses, they cannot be realized without cooperation among riparian states and thus form part of an overall obligation to cooperate, as will be considered next.

2.1.3 Duty to Cooperate

Articulated in Article 8 of the UNWC, the duty to cooperate obliges states to cooperate on the basis of sovereign equality, territorial integrity, mutual benefit, and good faith to attain optimal utilization and adequate protection of an international watercourse. The specific obligations of this duty are somewhat ambiguous. As noted by McCaffrey, 'it is of little use to speak of an "obligation to cooperate" in the abstract',[75] the general duty to cooperate should be viewed as an overarching term for a number of individual rights and duties detailed in procedural obligations, such as the obligation to exchange data and information. Leb explains that it is therefore possible for states to comply with the duty to cooperate in a number of different ways including 'through compliance with customary obligations that arise from the general duty and through other unilateral acts of [a] cooperative nature and mutual engagement in negotiations, consultations, planning and joint management'.[76] For the purposes of

73 Rio Declaration, *supra* note 71, Principle 2.
74 See *Pulp Mills*, *supra* note 64.
75 S. C. McCaffrey, *The Law of International Watercourses* (2nd ed., Oxford: OUP, 2007) 470.
76 C. Leb, *Cooperation in the Law of Transboundary Water Resources* (Cambridge: Cambridge University Press, 2013) 81.

this monograph it is also important to note that the substantive content of the duty to cooperate is found in the need to attain 'optimal and sustainable utilization', which, as has already been mentioned, is the goal of Article 5 pertaining to equitable and reasonable use. To enable holistic governance of natural resources, cooperation is key not only within one sector, but across all of those sectors that exist in different territorial jurisdictions and which may impact the resources. The WEF nexus and the SDGs can supplement or expand on the duty to cooperate as it exists within IWL to look to the energy and food sectors, as well as towards the fulfilment of global goals in the SDGs. For this to happen, cooperation must be accompanied by relevant methods of implementation, which are contained within the procedural provisions.

2.1.4 Procedural Provisions

While equitable and reasonable use, the no-harm rule and the duty to cooperate broadly make up the body of substantive norms, the UNWC also details a number of procedural norms that provide guidance to states on how to implement substantive obligations and promote cooperation. These norms include the obligation to notify and to consult on the potential effects of such planned measures, as well the exchange of data and information.[77] These rules are normally introduced in water treaty arrangements as a means of implementing substantive principles. While some procedural provisions have been argued to be binding upon all states as part of customary international law, this notion is controversial.[78] In the *Pulp Mills* case, the ICJ underlined that 'informing, notifying and negotiating constitute an appropriate means'[79] to realise the duty to cooperate when shared water resources are at stake. However, while it is commonplace to draw a linear division between the substantive and procedural rules of IWL,[80] the line is not clear cut. The principle of equitable and reasonable use and no significant harm require looking to the body of procedural rules to add further understanding and definition to the meaning of the substantive rules themselves.[81] As described by Leb:

77 See UNWC, *supra* note 2, Arts 11–19.

78 McCaffrey, '*The Customary Law of International Watercourses*', *supra* note 34.

79 *Pulp Mills*, *supra* note 64, para 81.

80 For instance, the majority of textbooks or research handbooks focusing on IWL divide chapters by substantive and procedural rules, see A. Rieu-Clarke, A. Allan & S. Hendry (Eds.), *Routledge Handbook of Water Law and Policy* (London and New York: Routledge, 2017).

81 Leb, *Cooperation in the Law of Transboundary Water Resources*, *supra* note 76, at 109.

> The doctrinal distinction between procedural and substantive rules of international water law that is observed by many authors facilitates schematisation for analytical purposes, yet it is a simplified conception of the nature of the rules of cooperation.

Wouters also notes that the duty to cooperate can act as a bridge between substantive and procedural obligations since cooperation obligations are made up of both substantive and procedural content.[82] The duty to cooperate requires states to work together towards the achievement of an equitable and reasonable allocation of uses and benefits from a watercourse (substantive) through information sharing which subsequently leads to consultations and negotiations (procedural). In this sense, the duty to cooperate can be seen as an umbrella which covers all of the duties contained within IWL.

International water conventions may adopt different approaches on the way in which procedures are introduced and formulated. For example, there are a number of differences between the procedural obligations of the UNWC and the UNECE Water Convention. Firstly, while the UNWC states that it does not affect existing agreements, only encouraging states to harmonise existing agreements with the provisions of the treaty,[83] the UNECE Water Convention obligates states to revise agreements in line with the Convention and 'eliminate contradictions'.[84] The UNECE Water Convention also goes further than the UNWC in its requirement for states to establish joint bodies; however, this is somewhat matched by the more elaborate provisions of the UNWC in relation to notification and consultation over 'planned measures'. Once again, the two conventions can therefore be seen as complementary, acting as one normative framework.

To recap, this sub-section has detailed the key principles of IWL; the principle of equitable and reasonable use, the duty to prevent significant harm, the duty to cooperate and procedural norms, all of which were built over more than 40 years of negotiations. The following two sub-sections will look at the policy framework of the WEF nexus and the development agenda of the SDGs. It is worth noting that the status of each of these instruments is completely different from the international treaties we have considered so far; they differ in the

82 P. Wouters, S. Vinogradov, A. Allan et al., *Sharing Transboundary Waters: An Integrated Assessment of Equitable Entitlement: The Legal Assessment Model*, IHP-VI, Technical Documents in Hydrology No. 74 (Paris: UNESCO, 2005), at 178. See also P. Okowa, '*Procedural Obligations in International Environmental Agreements*', 67:1, British Yearbook of International Law (1996) 275–336, 277.

83 UNWC, *supra* note 2, Art. 3.

84 UNECE, *Guide to Implementing the Water Convention*, *supra* note 37 at para 241.

extent to which they are legally binding, but importantly also in their political influence. This difference is what provides strength to the frameworks when utilized together in the LNG approach, as will be explained in Section 3.

2.2 *Water-Energy-Food Nexus*

Increased population growth and progressive urbanization across the globe has led to recognition of the growing pressures on the demand for water, energy and food, as well as the relationship between these sectors and resources. As a result, the WEF nexus was introduced during the 2008 World Economic Forum annual meeting which sought to develop 'understanding of how water is linked to economic growth across a nexus of issues'.[85] It has been defined or described as 'an approach to consider the interactions between water, food and energy, while taking into account the synergies and trade-offs that arise from the management of these three resources, and potential areas of conflict'.[86] The WEF nexus has since become a well-established paradigm within legal, scientific and policy literature.[87]

Interactions across the WEF nexus are numerous, for instance the treatment and distribution of water for drinking supply purposes is highly energy intensive; water is also a necessary component of energy production processes, such as cooling, mining, or hydropower generation. Similarly, energy is required for agricultural production and processing, and countries across the world increasingly are developing crops for biofuels as an energy source.[88] All of these competing uses can necessitate trade-offs being made between different sectors. As such, the WEF nexus has traditionally been framed around notions of security, relating to each of the relevant sectors.[89] However, with an understanding of the interrelated nature of water, energy and food, opportunities are also presented for better water resource management, which can be beneficial across all sectors. It is for this reason that the WEF nexus has become known as an important method for framing global development issues concerning

85 Pahl-Wostl, Bhaduri & Bruns, *supra* note 30.

86 S. Reinhard, J. Verhagen, W. Wolters & R. Ruben, *Water-Food-Energy-Nexus: A Quick Scan* (Wageningen: Wageningen Economic Research, 2017), https://edepot.wur.nl/424551, accessed 10 April 2020.

87 D. Waughray (Ed.), *Water Security: The Water-Food-Energy-Climate Nexus: The World Economic Forum Water Initiative* (Washington, DC: Island Press 2011), http://www3.weforum.org/docs/WEF_WI_WaterSecurity_WaterFoodEnergyClimateNexus_2011.pdf, accessed 11 May 2020, at xvii.

88 See 'Potential Future Impacts of Increased Biofuels Use', World Bank blogs, https://blogs.worldbank.org/developmenttalk/potential-future-impacts-of-increased-biofuels-use, accessed 1 June 2019.

89 Terrapon-Pfaff et al., *supra* note 23.

natural resources, moving away from the conventional policy approach of decision-making in topical 'silos'.[90] It is important to note that each sector within the WEF nexus has multifaceted concerns beyond mere resource utilization. Each sector produces and manages resources to increase and maintain a certain quality of life for human populations; as such, social development and human well-being are at the centre of the WEF nexus. Each sector is also supported and maintained by the environment and ecosystems that natural resources depend on for their sustainability. The WEF nexus is therefore concerned not only with water, food and energy but also with issues such as social inequality, environmental impact and economic volatility.[91]

The WEF nexus is not without criticism,[92] particularly with regard to its lack of specificity. It has been described as having traits of a 'nirvana concept',[93] defined by Molle as those that 'embody an ideal image of what the world should tend to. They represent a vision of a "horizon" that individuals and societies should strive to reach'.[94] However, as stated by Muller, it is 'increasingly widely recognised that no single organisational architecture can serve the diversity of water management situations'.[95] Thus, while taking a critical stance on the WEF nexus with reference to its lack of 'rigour and coherence', Muller ultimately concludes that the WEF paradigm succeeds in shifting focus of water management from 'watersheds to problem-sheds', more directly aligned to the needs and focus of governments, business and citizens.[96] The framing of the WEF nexus is important in this respect, developed from a perspective of business and industry and concerned with the achievement of water, food and energy security. However, as the WEF nexus has developed,

---

90 Waughray, *supra* note 87.

91 H. Hoff, *Understanding the Nexus. Background Paper for the Bonn 2011 Conference: The Water, Energy and Food Security Nexus* (Stockholm: Stockholm Environment Institute, 2011), https://mediamanager.sei.org/documents/Publications/SEI-Paper-Hoff-UnderstandingTheNexus-2011.pdf, accessed 10 May 2020.

92 G. B. Simpson & G. P. W. Jewitt, '*The Development of the Water-Energy-Food Nexus as a Framework for Achieving Resource Security: A Review*', 7, Frontiers in Environmental Science (2019). DOI:10.3389/fenvs.2019.00008; D. Wichelns, '*The Water-Energy-Food Nexus: Is the Increasing Attention Warranted, from Either a Research or Policy Perspective?*', 69, Environmental Science and Policy (2017) 113–123.

93 C. Middleton, J. Allouche, D. Gyawali & S. Allen, '*The Rise and Implications of the Water-Energy-Food Nexus in Southeast Asia through an Environmental Justice Lens*', 8:2, Water Alternatives (2015) 627–654.

94 F. Molle, '*Nirvana Concepts, Narratives and Policy Models: Insight from the Water Sector*', 1:1, Water Alternatives (2008) 131–156.

95 Muller, *supra* note 30, at 689.

96 *Id.*

security terminology has progressively been replaced by language of sustainable development.[97] This progression can be viewed positively in light of its alignment with global development at a larger scale while recognizing that the WEF nexus alone cannot be viewed as a comprehensive strategy. As argued by Allouche et al., a number of limitations exist when viewing the WEF nexus as an ideal system of optimization:

> It treats the trade-offs between human needs for water, energy and food as a perfect equilibrium model, in which resource allocation can be decided. This can encourage the commodification of resources, downplaying environmental externalities, such as biodiversity and climate change, as well as poverty alleviation needs, ignoring day-to-day realities, local priorities and needs.[98]

Allouche et al. stress the need for the WEF nexus to embrace inclusiveness, going beyond the three sectors of which its name is derived.[99]

It must also be noted that a power imbalance has persisted between the sectors with economic interests vested in energy and agriculture dominating the narrative and, in some instances, overpowering any notions of equitable and sustainable utilization of watercourses. It is therefore necessary to move away from the traditionally vertical structures of governance within each of the WEF sectors. Emphasis must be placed on improving the interconnectedness between frameworks, rather than forming new ones. As stated by Bazilian et al. the likelihood of communication failure between the WEF sectors is high given that there are extremely few experts on all three areas.[100] The authors also acknowledge that multisectoral complexities require the creation of a framework that is 'capable of abstracting the issues at appropriate levels for decision-making'.[101] Furthermore, the lack of normative structures within the nexus could be an issue when asking about implementation and weight of the standards of behaviour expected from it. The backing of existing frameworks such as IWL and the SDGs could breathe new life into the WEF nexus and provide a better understanding of the interdependencies between key areas.

---

97 Pahl-Wostl, *supra* note 17.

98 J. Allouche, C. Middleton & D. Gyawali, '*Technical Veil, Hidden Politics: Interrogating the Power Linkages behind the Nexus*', 8, Water Alternatives (2015) 610–626, at 617.

99 *Id.*, at 622.

100 M. Bazilian, H. Rogner, M. Howells et al., '*Considering the Energy, Water and Food Nexus: Towards an Integrated Modelling Approach*', 39, Energy Policy (2011) 7896–7906.

101 *Id.*, at 7898.

2.3 *Sustainable Development Goals*

SDG 6, the water goal, commits to '[e]nsure availability and sustainable management of water and sanitation for all'. Its subsequent targets cover all aspects of water governance, including 'universal and equitable access', which pays homage to the implementation of the human right to water, the need to 'improve water equality' and 'increase water-use efficiency', as well as protecting and restoring water-related ecosystems. In direct relation to governance, target 6.5 calls for the implementation of 'integrated water resources management at all levels, including through transboundary cooperation'. This target, while important for its significance in highlighting the need for integrated governance across sectors, is arguably outdated in the landscape of water governance. As mentioned at the outset of this monograph, IWRM has come under criticism for its lack of enforcement and its continued water centrism.[102] Its inclusion within the SDGs could therefore be viewed as a missed opportunity to develop a more progressive and inclusive approach that measures advancements in a number of ways, rather than on IWRM alone. The indicators by which target 6.5 is measured are the 'degree of integrated water resources management' (indicator 6.5.1)[103] and the 'proportion of transboundary basin area with an operational arrangement for water cooperation' (indicator 6.5.2). For such an arrangement to be deemed operational there must be existence of a joint body that has regular, formal communication between riparian countries (at least once per year), joint or coordinated management plans or objects, and regular exchange of data and information (at least once per year).[104] Emphasis is therefore clearly placed on cooperation through institutional structures. Yet, there are many different forms of cooperation, and it may be the case that less formal mechanisms are in place and well-functioning, but do not fall within the scope of the indicator.

The SDGs continue the siloed approach that has developed within international environmental governance more generally by dividing goals by sector and providing little illustration of the known overlaps and synergies between the goals. Ambitious targets, such as doubling agricultural productivity, increasing renewable energy and improving water quality, are in place across each of the WEF sectors. Three of the SDGs relate specifically to the WEF nexus: water (SDG 6), energy (SDG 7) and food (SDG 2). Each of the goals are undoubtedly linked; resource management (particularly within the water sector) will

102 Benson, Gain & Rouillard, *supra* note 22.

103 For further details on monitoring target 6.5.1, see Bertule et al., *supra* note 18.

104 UN-Water, *Integrated Monitoring Guide for Sustainable Development Goal 6 on Water and Sanitation: Targets and Global Indicators* (Geneva: UN-Water, 14 July 2017), https://www.unwater.org/publications/sdg-6-targets-indicators/, accessed 10 May 2020.

be essential for the achievement of each goal, as will the necessary political will and cooperative framework. This interconnectedness provides scope for the establishment of synergies and mutual supportiveness, but also gives rise to the risk of trade-offs being made through the prioritization of one goal over another.

SDG 2 aims to end hunger, achieve food security, improve nutrition and promote sustainable agriculture. While no specific reference to water is made within the goal or its subsequent targets, reference to sustainable agriculture and 'resilient agricultural practices' can be related to the need to utilise water resources in the most efficient way possible.[105] SDG 7 focuses on ensuring access to affordable, reliable, sustainable and modern energy for all. Its subsequent targets and indicators relate to increasing the share of renewable energy and doubling the global rate of improvement in energy efficiency. Once again, no reference is made to water (or indeed to other natural resources) within the goal, despite there being clear links between renewable energy and water resources, particularly in relation to hydropower.[106]

In 2016, the UN Water Task Force provided a first evaluation of the interlinkages of SDG 6 with the other SDGs.[107] By focusing on the three pillars of sustainable development: social, economic and environmental, the brief illustrates the complexity of the SDGs and highlights the cross-cutting nature of their implementation. With regard to SDG 2, the report demonstrates the link between SDG 6 and ending hunger by providing nutritious and sufficient food all year round, ending all forms of malnutrition, doubling agricultural productivity and ensuring sustainable food production systems and resilient agricultural practices.[108] It highlights that these linkages are social in character. With regards to SDG 7, the report recognises the relationship with SDG 6 and the achievement of universal access to modern energy services, increased shares of renewable energy and the doubling of energy efficiency.[109] The report notes that energy is critical for economic development

105 SDGs, *supra* note 1, Goal 2, Target 2.4.

106 *Id.*, Goal 7. Notably specific reference is made to least developed countries and landlocked developing countries within Target 7.b.

107 UN-Water, *Water and Sanitation Interlinkages across the 2030 Agenda for Sustainable Development* (Geneva: UN-Water, 2016), http://www.unwater.org/publications/water-sanitation-interlinkages-across-2030-agenda-sustainable-development/, accessed 10 May 2020.

108 *Id.*, 20, Table 1: Targets of SDG Goal 2.

109 *Id.*, at 26, Table 2.

but stresses that increasing fossil-fuel based energy can increase demands on water. It further states that some renewable energy, such as hydropower and bioenergy can also have 'significant impacts on land and water resources and ecosystems' and states that 'care should be taken to minimize these impacts'.[110] Furthermore, both SDGs 2 and 7 are discussed with regard to the relationship with SDG 6 in an environmental sense.[111] This interdependency between the goals was also discussed at the 2016 Budapest Water Summit Statement, where water was considered as a connector of various SDGs, highlighting the role of resources, such as international watercourses, for the attainment of SDGs across multiple sectors.[112]

Authors and international bodies have also discussed this crucial symbiotic relationship between the SDGs. The UN World Water Assessment Programme illustrated that target 6.3, which focuses on improving water quality by reducing pollution, eliminating dumping and minimizing the release of hazardous chemicals, could challenge SDG 7 on energy as the collection of wastewater requires a significant amount of energy.[113] In addition, this target is also likely to be financially burdensome on countries that do not have sufficient financial resources or technology available. Nilsson et al. have provided a systematic way for policy-makers to view the interactions between the targets by using a seven-point scale to view those which are inextricably linked to the achievement of another (indivisible) or if targets clash (counteracting).[114] The relationship between SDG 6 and 16 has also been highlighted by Orme et al. who suggest that the goals should be addressed together in order to ensure a holistic interpretation and implementation of the SDGs.[115] Further, SDG 13, to 'take urgent action to combat climate change and its impacts', is vital to bear in mind across all of the SDGs. Climate change will impact transboundary water resources in many ways, particularly within countries that are already prone

---

110 *Id.*, at 25.

111 *Id.*, at 28.

112 World Water Council, '*Messages and Policy Recommendations*', Budapest Water Summit, 28–30 November 2016 (Budapest: Ministry of Foreign Affairs and Trade of Hungary, 2016).

113 United Nations World Water Assessment Programme (WWAP), *The United Nations World Water Development Report 2017: Wastewater, The Untapped Resource* (Paris: UNESCO, 2017), https://www.unwater.org/publications/world-water-development-report-2017/, accessed 10 May 2020.

114 M. Nilsson, D. Griggs & M. Visbeck, '*Policy: Map the Interactions between Sustainable Development Goals*', 534, Nature (2016) 320–322.

115 Orme et al., *supra* note 23.

to drought.[116] Therefore, climate impacts need to be taken into consideration within the formation of any governance framework.[117]

As has been demonstrated, there is no shortage of literature illustrating the interlinkages between the SDGs. However, the majority of this literature exists within the political or scientific sphere and therefore does not relate to legal commitments. More importantly, the attainment of the SDGs relevant to this monograph, in relation to the use and conservation of international watercourses, face two challenges: first, fierce competition among riparian states over water resources in order to achieve goals nationally, which has the potential to result in conflict. Secondly, even if it is assumed that the SDGs do not cause conflict *per se* and recognizing their essential role in inspiring the international community to effect change in society, the achievement of the goals by one or more countries may come at the expense of others. While basin-wide cooperation and management can be found among the indicators of the SDGs, this does not negate the possibility of prosperity of one country being detrimental to another as the SDGs alone are not designed to promote equitable and reasonable use of water resources among riparian states. If the SDGs are supplemented by legal frameworks such as IWL and holistic paradigms such as the WEF, the likelihood of their achievement may be improved, while risks of trade-offs are potentially mitigated or even eliminated.

3 The LNG Approach: towards Integration

In order to balance the friction between different sectors and countries and minimise economic losses from inefficiency, a streamlined and holistic approach to water governance should be taken. Both horizontal and vertical integration is needed within governance frameworks, working from the local to international level and across a multitude of sectors. The UNWC finds its direction as a result of decades of negotiations, largely surrounding debates on sovereignty over watercourses and thus relates to the interstate relationship of water resources. The WEF nexus can be traced to the need to recognise the trade-offs made across multiple sectors and industries, particularly as a result of economic growth and population increase, finding its foundation within science and economics. The SDGs predominately focus on accessibility to water

116 See L. Oyebande & S. Odunuga, '*Climate Change Impact on Water Resources at the Transboundary Level in West Africa: The Cases of the Senegal, Niger and Volta Basins*', 4, The Open Hydrology Journal (2010) 163–172.

117 T. Honkonen, '*Water Security and Climate Change: The Need for Adaptive Governance*', 20, Potchefstroom Electronic Law Journal (2017).

resources, as well as food and energy security, developed from a more anthropocentric perspective through the prism of international development. Each of these perspectives bring different approaches to governance and diverse lessons which can be disseminated into one relatively cohesive framework: the LNG approach.

3.1 *Overview of Approach*

Section 2 provided a basic understanding of IWL, the WEF nexus and the SDGs. It has been demonstrated that while each of the frameworks have significant strengths, weaknesses also exist. Each of the three frameworks is well recognized by the international community, but each for different reasons and with varied status regarding implementation. While the UNWC has struggled to gain support in terms of ratifications, its principles are widely recognized as part of customary international law.[118] In addition, despite ratifications of the Convention itself being few (still only 37 as of July 2020), its key principles have been replicated in other regional or basin-scale frameworks, as will be demonstrated in the discussion on the ZRB in Section 4 below. Yet, the nature of the UNWC as a framework convention, while allowing states scope to tailor its provisions to their own needs, has also resulted in vague provisions that lack specificity and relatability for watercourse states, resulting in failure or difficulty in fulfilling legal obligations.

In comparison, the WEF nexus seeks a balance between achieving water, energy and food security; goals which are better understood and aimed for by all national governments, particularly within a developing country context. However, the strong legal force of the UNWC can be contrasted by the WEF nexus, which, since its inception in 2011 has been used within scientific and policy literature but has been largely absent from legal discussions. This is despite the UNECE Water Convention issuing a WEF methodology to demonstrate the importance of the WEF nexus for sustainable water governance.[119] The WEF has therefore been utilized in a niche way and has not received the level of uptake required to mitigate potential trade-offs between each of the water, energy and food sectors. On the other hand, the SDGs, like the MDGs before them, have garnered enormous international support, likely as a result of their

118 See Dellapenna, *supra* note 47.

119 UNECE, 'The Nexus Methodology', http://www.unece.org/?id=43460, accessed 12 April 2020. See also, UNECE, *Methodology for Assessing the Water-Food-Energy-Ecosystem Nexus in Transboundary Basins and Experiences from its Application: Synthesis* (New York and Geneva: United Nations, 2018), http://www.unece.org/fileadmin/DAM/env/water/publications/WAT_55_NexusSynthesis/ECE-MP-WAT-55_NexusSynthesis_Final-for-Web.pdf, accessed 12 April 2020.

'soft law' non-binding status and global political pressure.[120] But aiming for each individual goal and target in silos, in addition to working towards fulfilling obligations presented by other frameworks, is a complex task requiring significant capacity, which may be out with the reach of many developing countries. As such, integrating the SDGs and the WEF nexus to add flesh to and implement the key principles of IWL could serve as a holistic framework to aid the effectiveness of water governance. The LNG approach would bring together state-centred international law, the science-driven nexus and the goals and aspirations of the international community.

3.2 *Interpreting and Implementing IWL*

The basic thesis of this monograph, as indicated in various sections thus far, is that the implementation of IWL could be aided by its incorporation with the WEF nexus and SDGs. While the law is instrumental in the governance of transboundary watercourses, the two frameworks add further strength to the UNWC and IWL more generally. The following sections will demonstrate how the WEF nexus and SDGs can aid the implementation of IWL by adding further substance to key legal principles. As the cardinal rule of IWL, equitable and reasonable use will be examined in detail, with specific analysis of many of the factors contained in Article 6.

3.2.1 Equitable and Reasonable Use

Regardless of the way in which equitable and reasonable use is interpreted, it remains ambiguous. This level of uncertainty complicates judgements and makes the application of a principle around water equity difficult.[121] As stated by Lankford, having 'numerous countries in a transboundary basin with numerous criteria leads to mathematical equality rather than jurisprudential equity. It is this misdirection that could potentially create unnecessary contention amongst riparians'.[122] Lankford also argues that Article 6, while vague in some ways, is actually too detailed in others. He notes that the provision contains guiding words by stating 'requires taking into account all relevant factors and circumstances', this is followed by too many factors and the words 'weight to be given to each factor'; all of this, he argues, provides a degree of prescription

120 For discussion of 'soft' power in relation to transboundary watercourses, particularly in the case of hegemonic political contexts, see M. Zeitoun, N. Mirumachi & J. Warner, '*Transboundary Water Interaction II: The Influence of "Soft" Power*', 11, International Environmental Agreements: Politics, Law and Economics (2011) 159–178.

121 A. M. Onencan & B. V. Van de Walle, '*Equitable and Reasonable Utilization: Reconstructing the Nile Basin Water Allocation Dialogue*', 10:6, Water (Switzerland) (2018) 2.

122 Lankford, *supra* note 43, at 139.

and method which may take participants towards mathematically equal outcomes.[123] Lankford suggests alterations could be made, such as changing wording to 'factors shall be taken into account' or 'multiple approaches to water allocation shall be taken into account'. However, while removing potentially prescriptive texts and increasing flexibility of implementation may be helpful, the main difficulty with the provisions on equitable and reasonable use is their lack of practical guidance. Indeed, attempts to add more substance to the provisions of equitable and reasonable use are not new. Van de Zaag attempted to put together a number of measurable criteria for defining the allocation of water in an equitable manner,[124] while Wouters et al. attempted to create more detailed metrics to inform water cooperation through their Legal Assessment Model.[125] However, considering the period of time needed to reach agreement on the UNWC itself, it is not likely that a consensus could be reached regarding amendments to the text of equitable and reasonable use. Instead, attempts must be made to look beyond IWL to additional frameworks, including WEF nexus and the SDGs, to aid the implementation of key principles such as equitable and reasonable use.

Integration of other key water uses (such as energy and food) give meaning to factors such as existing and future uses of the watercourse vis-à-vis development, particularly as such developments are likely to impact each aspect of the WEF nexus. Such developments will also have an impact on the achievement of the SDGs; building hydropower dams may, for example, add to progress towards the achievement of SDG 7 on energy. It could, at the same time, fail to ensure that the watercourse continues to protect an existing ecosystem, or indeed, sustain the livelihoods of populations dependant on it, resulting in poor progress towards SDG target 6.6 to 'protect and restore' water-related ecosystems and Goal 1 which aims to end poverty in all its form everywhere. Without taking a holistic perspective which incorporates these frameworks, it is possible that governments will see trade-offs that may be of a higher magnitude than necessary. In light of this, the following subsections will illustrate how exactly the LNG approach could reinforce and clarify the factors of equitable and reasonable use in particular.

3.2.2 Factors of Equitable and Reasonable Use

The list of factors listed under Article 6 is not exhaustive and their consideration will vary on a case-by-case basis as each international watercourse has a

123 *Id.*

124 Van Der Zaag, Seyam & Savenije, *supra* note 42.

125 Wouters et al., *supra* note 82.

variety of natural and man-made characteristics.[126] Understanding and applying the factors could be enriched by using the WEF nexus and the SDGs to reconcile a number of different—and often competing—uses of international watercourses. An LNG approach to each of the factors is provided in the following sections.

3.2.2.1 *Natural Characteristics*

The first factor considers 'geographic, hydrographic, hydrological, climatic, ecological and other factors of a natural character'.[127] The WEF nexus can link to these natural characteristics when taking into account the different strengths and weaknesses of each watercourse state. For instance, the geographical character of two watercourse states may make one much more suited to irrigation for food production, while another may be better suited to utilization of the watercourse for hydropower development. These key differences often link to the location of a watercourse based on its positioning in terms of being upstream or downstream on the watercourse, and thereby its use of the watercourse is determined by the flow of water.[128] Similarly, although SDG 6 does not refer to such natural factors, it expressly recognizes climate change effects on access to water of countries and populations. If this is read in conjunction with Goal 13 (climate action), which refers to the 'human impact of geo-physical disasters', one appreciates the need 'to integrate disaster risk measures, sustainable natural resource management … into national development strategies'. This is clearly relevant to the question of equity in the context of managing international watercourses. Natural characteristics can also be impacted by water uses, as stated by Leb:

> [Natural characteristics] can affect another state's physical territory, for example through flow velocity changes that impact riverbed stability and the geomorphology of the river, or reduction of flood risk and damage through flow regulation. They can affect existing uses or foreclose future water development opportunities in other parts of the basin, for

126 For more details see L. Caflisch, '*Equitable and Reasonable Utilisation and Factors Relevant to Determining Such Utilisation* (*Articles 5 and 6*)', in Boisson de Chazournes et al., *supra* note 2, 77–94.

127 *Id.*, at 85–86.

128 The positioning of watercourse states has often formed the basis of their opinions with regard to the provisions of the UNWC in relation to concerns over limitations of sovereignty regarding use of the watercourse. See Salman, '*The United Nations Watercourses Convention Ten Years Later*', *supra* note 57.

> instance by changing the hydropower potential downstream through upstream development. These impacts may cause harm, or they may be beneficial.[129]

Thus, the state of natural characteristics is not permanent. Considerations of this factor need to be flexible and adaptive and continuously evaluated during any development initiatives. Inclusion of the WEF nexus allows expansion into two of the sectors most likely to result in a change to natural characteristics, while the scope of the SDGs integrates processes of risk management that are likely to otherwise remain absent.

3.2.2.2 *Social and Economic Needs*

Article 6(1)(b) provides that the 'social and economic needs of the watercourse states concerned' must be taken into account in determining what is equitable and reasonable. This factor requires decision-makers to understand the importance of distributing resource utilization and balancing trade-offs to meet the socio-economic demands of those uses.[130] This should include taking into consideration the level of economic development and priorities relating to food and energy security while continuing to ensure the protection of the watercourse. It is not clear from the provision how socio-economic criteria should be evaluated, or whether pertinent uses should be distinguished from non-pertinent uses.[131]

This factor can also be linked to Article 6(1)(c) which relates to the population dependant on the watercourse.[132] Population dependency should not be considered solely in terms of the number of people living within the watercourse, but also based on the characteristics of that population. For instance, the requirements of a dense population within an urban area on a watercourse versus that of rural pastoralists would be very different. In this sense, a simplistic perspective of the number of people dependant on the watercourse is not sufficient, links must be made to their social and economic needs,

---

129 C. Leb, '*One Step at a Time: International Law and the Duty to Cooperate in the Management of Shared Water Resources*', 40, Water International (2014) 21–32, 21.

130 For further analysis of socio-economic need as a criterion for equitableness, see *Delimitation of the Maritime Boundary in the Gulf of Maine Area (Canada v United States)*, [1984] ICJ Rep 165.

131 See X. Fuentes, '*The Criteria for the Equitable Utilization of International Rivers*', 67:1, The British Yearbook of International Law (1997) 337–412.

132 Water use increases at more than twice the rate of population growth, see Leb, '*One Step at a Time*', *supra* note 129, at 21.

including access to and affordability of resources. Interpretation of social and economic needs will be shaped by the relations that exist within the region and the country itself in relation to geographical and geopolitical considerations. In this respect, the WEF nexus offers a distinct approach to the critical issues that countries face with respect to food, energy and other vital uses of water. Not only quantifying and determining those needs, but also proposing potential trade-offs between such different uses of water resources, could be an important additional tool to determine what is equitable or not in light of other factors.

Cases considered by the ICJ have demonstrated reluctance to tackle socio-economic issues. However, some consideration has been given to socio-economic need in maritime delimitation cases.[133] There is a close relationship between border disputes and transboundary watercourses.[134] Thus, while cases may not be about international watercourses, lessons can be learned from the way that courts have considered similar factors in such cases, particularly when they deal with resource issues and principles such as equity. In the *North Sea Continental Shelf* cases,[135] the ICJ stated that its task was to look at delimitation, not the apportionment of the concerned area.[136] This reluctance is likely to be founded in the sensitivity around social and economic status of states concerned. In spite of this, the *Gulf of Maine* case did give some consideration to the economic dependence of coastal communities when determining the equitability of delimitation.[137]As noted by Fuentes, although the case did not use economic dependence as a factor for determining the delimitation line, it 'used it as an auxiliary criterion to verify the chosen line did not entail catastrophic repercussions to the livelihood and economic well-being of the costal population of the States concerned'.[138] This consideration of the significance of the natural resource to the livelihood of citizens concerned is testament to the importance of socio-economic factors.

In the *Jan Mayen* case, the Court, while expressly rejecting giving attention to socio-economic factors, took account of equitable access to the fishery resources present in the area.[139] In contrast, in the *Tunisia/Libya* case, the ICJ,

133 Fuentes, *supra* note 131.

134 See S. McCaffrey, '*Introductory Remarks: The Last Drop: Practical Tools for Addressing Transboundary Water Crises*', in *Proceedings of the 113th ASIL Annual Meeting* (Cambridge: Cambridge University Press, 2019) 313–329, at 315.

135 *North Sea Continental Shelf Cases* (*Federal Republic of Germany/Denmark; Federal Republic of Germany/Netherlands*), Judgment (Merits), [1969] ICJ Rep 3.

136 *Id.*, at 22, para 18.

137 *Gulf of Maine*, *supra* note 130, at 77–78, para 107.

138 Fuentes, *supra* note 131, at 342.

139 *Case Concerning Maritime Delimitation in the Area between Greenland and Jan Mayen* (*Denmark v. Norway*), [1993] ICJ Rep 38, at 71–72, paras 75, 76, 80.

referring to the unpredictability of natural fortune vis-à-vis natural resources argued that '[a] country might be poor today and become rich tomorrow as a result of an event such as the discovery of a valuable economic resource'.[140] The statement was made in relation to an argument made by Tunisia regarding its relative poverty in comparison to Libya in relation to natural resources. The problem highlighted by the Court is the temporal nature of socio-economic factors and their ability to change rapidly. While notable, this argument is reduced by the fact that each of the factors considered within Article 6 are evolutionary in nature; none of them relate to the consideration of an aspect of the watercourse that is permanent. The difficulty is not, therefore, whether social and economic need should be considered, but rather *how* they should be considered, as noted by Fuentes:

> [T]he real objection to the inclusion of socio-economic factors does not lie in a *per se* extra-legal nature of the socio-economic criteria, but on *how* these factors should operate in the process of delimitation so that the decision does not intrude into the political realm.[141]

The same point can be extended to the equitable and reasonable use of watercourses vis-à-vis social and economic need. The WEF nexus can once again provide additional information that can be used to add substance to the consideration of this factor. Energy and food security are primary concerns within a number of the countries which share international watercourses.[142] Indeed, many conflicts concerning transboundary basins relate not to the social and economic benefits derived from the watercourse *per se*, but from the benefits that can be gained from its utilization, such as irrigation for food production or hydropower developments. The need for development in these two areas is vital for many developing countries. Thus, a holistic demonstration of the social and economic need relating to, not only water, but also to energy and food would provide a more rounded image of the development needs of riparian countries.

This development must, of course, still be met with the caveat of equitable and reasonable use and sustainable development. The SDGs can play a key role by linking to the achievement of SDGs 2 (food) and 7 (energy), but also

140 *Case Concerning the Continental Shelf between Tunisia and Libyan Arab Jamahiriya (Tunisia/Libyan Arab Jamahiriya)*, Judgment, [1982] ICJ Rep 18, at 77, para 107.

141 Fuentes, *supra* note 131, emphasis in original.

142 See UNECE, *Reconciling Resource Uses in Transboundary Basins: Assessment of the Water-Food-Energy-Ecosystems Nexus* (New York and Geneva: United Nations, 2015), http://www.unece.org/fileadmin/DAM/env/water/publications/WAT_46_Nexus/ece_mp.wat_46_eng.pdf, accessed 12 April 2020.

Goal 12, which focuses on sustainable consumption and production patterns, and Goal 10, which aims to reduce inequality within and among countries, as well as Goal 1 on ending poverty. In terms of social need, Goal 2 requires monitoring the prevalence of undernourishment (indicator 2.1.1) and malnutrition (indicator 2.2.2), as well as the proportion of agricultural area under productive and sustainable agriculture (indicator 2.4.1). Consideration of the social and economic need of states could therefore look at these indicators as demonstrations of social 'need' vis-à-vis food security. There is, of course, the potential for such schemes to also damage the potential to reach other targets, such as indicator 2.3.2 which looks at the income of small-scale food producers. Large-scale irrigation schemes have the potential to limit opportunities for small-scale farmers, demonstrating another area of analysis that the SDGs can draw importance to. The same is true of Goal 7 which provides indicators relating to the proportion of the population with access to electricity (indicator 7.1.1) as well as the proportion of renewable energy (indicators 7.1.2, 7.2.1 and 7.b.1). Hydropower developments clearly provide an opportunity to work towards the achievement of these goals, however, such developments must be balanced holistically with other goals, particularly those relating to reduced inequality between countries (Goal 10), as well as those with environmental focus, as described in relation to natural characteristics.

3.2.2.3 *Existing, Potential and Alternative Uses*

The uses of water and their efficiency is a focus within IWL, the WEF nexus and the SDGs. In relation to equitable and reasonable use, states are required to use and develop the watercourse 'with a view to attaining optimal and sustainable utilization'.[143] The use of 'optimal utilization' was the subject of controversy during drafting, raising concern that it may have economic connotations that could be used to give the most efficient user of an international watercourse priority over less technologically developed riparian states. As a result, the following information was provided during the drafting process:

> Attaining optimal utilization and benefits [of an international watercourse] did not mean achieving 'maximum' use or the most technologically efficient use or that the State capable of making the most efficient use of the watercourse should have superior claim to it. It meant the attainment of the best possible uses and benefits for all with a minimum of harm, in

143 UNWC, *supra* note 2, Art. 5(1).

> the light of all relevant circumstances and a manner consistent with the adequate protection of the watercourse in terms, for instance, of flood or pollution control.[144]

This detail is important when considering the existing, potential and alternative uses of watercourses as the technology deficit existing between countries also plays a significant role here. Efficient water use is a focus of both the SDGs, illustrated through target 6.4 and the UNWC Article 6(1)(f) relating to economy of use. Despite their inclusion within both frameworks, water efficiency has been demonstrated to be limited as a means of determining equitable utilization.[145] The nature of the efficiency requirement has been developed further in the *Colorado v. New Mexico* case.[146] The court explained that states have an 'affirmative duty to take reasonable steps to augment the water supply of an interstate stream'[147] and that they have 'a duty to employ "financially and physically feasible"' measures that are 'adapted to conserving and equalizing the natural flow'.[148] The reference to 'financially and physically feasible' demonstrates acknowledgement that while some other methods of utilization may be the most 'efficient', they may not be realistic within some contexts, particularly in relation to developing countries.

In many cases, existing uses will refer to requirements of irrigation or hydropower projects and therefore clearly links to the need to consider the WEF nexus. In the *Narmada Water Disputes* case, the tribunal took into account the extent of irrigable land, noting that this was one of the most important criteria to be considered.[149] In previous cases tribunals have also given preference to irrigated land, as opposed to irrigable land.[150] It is interesting to note that based on the wording of the factor itself, neither existing nor potential uses should be given preference, but should instead be treated equally. Thus, a fine

---

144 International Law Commission, '*Draft Articles on the Law of the Non-navigational Uses of International Watercourses and Commentaries Thereto and Resolution on Transboundary Confined Groundwater*', in *Report of the ILC on the Work of Its Forty-sixth Session (2 May–22 July 1994)*, UN Doc. A/49/10, at 97 [ILC Draft Articles].

145 Fuentes, *supra* note 131.

146 *Colorado v. New Mexico* (1982) 459 US 176.

147 *Id.*, at 185.

148 *Id.*

149 Government of India, *Report of the Narmada Water Disputes Tribunal* (New Delhi, 1979), Vol. I, http://cwc.gov.in/sites/default/files/NARMADA%20WATER%20DISPUTES%20TRIBUNAL-VOL-I.pdf, accessed 11 May 2020, at p. 137, para 9.5.1; p. 138, para 9.6.1.

150 Government of India, *Report of the Krishna Water Disputes Tribunal* (1973), Vol. II, at 172–174. http://www.cwc.gov.in/sites/default/files/KWDT-I_1973%20_volume2.pdf, accessed 24 July 2020.

balance has to be struck between existing uses and what the potential uses are, while ensuring that due recognition is given to the different development trajectories of each country. In this sense, considerations of existing, potential and alternative uses relate clearly to principles of both intra- and intergenerational equity.[151] Consideration of equity across the same generation also gives rise to discussions of 'fairness' and links to the aforementioned ideas of different meanings of optimal and sustainable utilization, based upon the financial and technical ability of the states involved.[152]

The UNECE *Guide to Implementing the Water Convention* also makes clear the link between intergenerational equity and the use of international watercourses; Article 2, paragraph 2(c) should be read in conjunction with Article 2, paragraph 5(c) according to which 'water resources shall be managed so that the needs of the present generation are met without compromising the ability of future generations to meet their own needs'.[153] This is fully in line with the contemporary developments of customary international law in relation to international watercourses, according to which the principle of equitable use incorporates that of sustainable development.[154] That is to say that a use of an international water body may not be considered as equitable, and therefore legal, if it is not sustainable. This is significant when considering developments on international watercourses as uses which may be economically viable to one state today, but not be viable to another for years to come.[155] Interpretation of this provision must therefore include an understanding of the key sectors and actors that play a major role within the basin, ensuring that governance regimes (and the implementation of IWL in particular) include taking an active part in consultation processes with stakeholders across all WEF sectors. Both the existing and future uses of the watercourse will be linked to national development plans and strategies formed at a national level and may be formed by a number of different government departments. By taking an LNG approach, a more cohesive strategy can be developed for the mapping

151 Intergenerational equity relates to equity between past and future generations. Intragenerational equity refers to equality between people of the same generation. See O. Spijkers, '*Intergenerational Equity and the Sustainable Development Goals*', 10:11, Sustainability (2018) 3836.

152 See Z. Yihdego, '*The Fairness "Dilemma" in Sharing the Nile Waters: What Lessons from the Grand Ethiopian Renaissance Dam for International Law?*', 2:2, Brill Research Perspectives in International Water Law (2017); Yihdego & Rieu-Clarke, *supra* note 16.

153 UNECE, *Guide to Implementing the Water Convention*, *supra* note 84, at 22.

154 See O. McIntyre, '*The Role of Customary Rules and Principles of International Environmental Law in the Protection of Shared International Freshwater Resources*', 46, Natural Resources Journal (2006) 157–210.

155 Spijkers, *supra* note 24, at 46.

of all existing, potential and alternative uses of watercourses and how they may (or may not) contribute to sustainable development and the achievement of intra- and intergenerational equity. Once again, this factor can clearly be linked to SDG 10, which aims to reduce inequality within and among states, and SDG 12, which targets sustainable consumption and production patterns.

3.2.2.4 *Conservation and Protection*

While some sense of 'watercourse protection' is included within Article 20 and 21 of the UNWC, environmental considerations are not strongly represented within Article 6.[156] In this sense, as stated by Burchi, it can be argued that the UNWC and its application have not really kept up with the 'greening' of water law.[157] While Article 20 does refer to the 'protection and preservation of ecosystems' of international watercourses; this protection and preservation is unlikely to occur through the framework of IWL alone. With regard to the implementation of this provision, authors such as McIntyre have considered the use of an 'ecosystem approach' as 'crucial to the effective realization of the fundamental objective of international water law'.[158] However, it is necessary to note that the UNWC was not born from the era of environmental focus; emphasis was placed on water quantity rather than quality. The same is not true of the UNECE Water Convention, which places greater emphasis on water quality and environmental matters. In the UNECE Water Convention equitable and reasonable use is carefully combined with the ecosystem approach, the precautionary principle, polluter pays and sustainable development principles. The Convention also requires the preparation of environmental impact assessments (Article 3, para 1(h)), the establishment of water quality objectives, adoption of water-quality criteria and the implementation of best practices for the reduction of nutrient and hazardous substance inputs from diffuse sources.

However, despite the lack of explicit reference within the provisions themselves, within its commentary to the UNWC, the ILC made it clear that ecosystems needed protection and preservation in order 'to ensure their continued viability as life support systems, thus providing an essential basis for sustainable development'.[159] These obligations can clearly be linked to SDG

156 Article 20 deals with the protection and preservation of ecosystems, while Article 21 covers the prevention, reduction and control of pollution.

157 S. Burchi, '*The Future of Domestic Water Law: Trends and Developments Revisited, and Where Reform Is Headed*', 44, Water International (2019) 258–277.

158 O. McIntyre '*Environmental Protection and the Ecosystem Approach*' in McCaffrey, Leb & Denoon, *supra* note 5, 126–146, at 129.

159 ILC Draft Articles, *supra* note 144, at 119.

target 6.6, which relates to the protection and restoration of water-related ecosystems, as well as SDG 15, which calls on states to 'ensure the conservation, restoration and sustainable use of freshwater ecosystems in line with obligations under international agreements'. Indicator 15.1.2 looks at the proportion of important sites for freshwater biodiversity that are covered by protected areas, while indicator 15.6.1 looks at the number of countries that have frameworks in place for the fair and equitable sharing of benefits. The incorporation of these indicators within any considerations of the conservation and protection of an international watercourse could allow an opportunity to work towards the achievement of such SDG indicators.

Further, by using a WEF nexus approach to the conservation and protection of international watercourses issues such as agricultural run-off and ecosystem changes as a result of altered water flow, or increased sedimentation due to large-scale development such as hydropower, can be considered. As will be discussed below regarding the duty to cooperate, one of the main difficulties with regard to international watercourses is a lack of sufficient data. Using the LNG approach could allow data to be shared across government departments such as agriculture, energy and water. This would create a comprehensive analysis of the uses of the watercourse, enhance potential planning to mitigate any potential trade-offs and strengthen synergies.

3.2.3 No Significant Harm

As previously noted, integration with the WEF nexus would allow additional input from other sectors to be used in the planning stages of development projects to be able to prevent significant harm. The expansion of evaluation to the water and energy sectors has the potential to reduce the chances of unforeseen significant harm arising in the aftermath of the project; in relation to trade-offs relating to other sectors. Interpretation of no significant harm through the lens of the WEF nexus also means taking into consideration any potential significant impacts on the food (agriculture) and energy (hydropower) industries. This link can also be aided by tying into the concept of intergenerational equity and sustainable development. As noted by Zeitoun, the relevance of IWL to later developing states has been questioned.[160] This is largely because developments may take place in states that are more developed, which limits the ability of other riparian states to develop at some stage in the future. However, analysis of IWL demonstrates that favour is not provided to either upstream or downstream states, whether early or later developing, but rather

160 M. Zeitoun, '*The Relevance of International Water Law to Later-developing Upstream States*', 40:7, Water International (2015) 949–968.

evaluates each development on a case-by-case basis. It is this evaluation which can be aided by the incorporation of additional sectoral uses of watercourses.

Within the SDGs, obligations that would normally be considered due diligence are placed within the context of sustainable development. In target 6.3, the reduction of pollution is linked to improved water quality and the recycling of water, not to the obligation not to cause harm. This would mean that no significant harm is going over and above a due diligence obligation, linking it to concepts of both inter- and intragenerational equity. As noted by Spijkers, Article 7 of the UNWC, the 'no harm rule', could be interpreted to mean no harm caused to both present and future generations, as well as to the environment itself, therefore moving beyond the inter-state paradigm of the no-harm rule and indeed of IWL as a whole.[161] While this view is a useful consideration, it is likely to be difficult to enforce due to transboundary watercourse uses being in a state of continuous flux. What is essential, therefore, is that frameworks are flexible and adaptive, as well as holistic in nature.

Evidence from the WEF nexus, either based upon single projects that have proven to be controversial or a mapping of the WEF nexus within an entire water system, can be used in considerations of what may result in 'significant harm'. These considerations can demonstrate impact across all three WEF sectors and allow states to take appropriate measures to prevent significant harm. This holistic perspective may help to mitigate or eliminate significant harm on the economy or environment of those who have been significantly affected by resorting to applying necessary trade-offs that are acceptable to all concerned. This is not to say that all ills and challenges of applying significant harm would be solved through the LNG approach, but consideration of 'harm' can be substantially strengthened in its determination and implementation.

3.2.4 Duty to Cooperate

Although cooperation or non-cooperation between riparian states is determined by various geopolitical and sovereignty factors, lack of scientific evidence and misunderstanding concerning the risks and benefits of energy, food or drinking water projects relating to a watercourse are often amongst the major causes of dispute or tension between riparian states. As stated by Subramanian et al. it is essential for cooperation on transboundary watercourses that perceived risks are mitigated as far as possible;[162] the expansion of IWL frameworks to the WEF nexus and SDGs has the potential to assist

161 Spijkers, *supra* note 24, at 45.

162 A. Subramanian, B. Brown & A. Wolf, '*Understanding and Overcoming Risks to Cooperation along Transboundary Rivers*', 16, Water Policy (2014) 824–843.

with this risk mitigation by opening up space for dialogue and cooperation across sectors, including multiple government agencies and regional authorities, as well as increasing stakeholder participation.[163] The integration of the WEF nexus broadens the scope for the inclusion of private sector and industry stakeholders as the nexus has historically been industry orientated; since its formation emphasis has been placed on public-private partnerships in order to transform the water sector.[164] Inclusion of the private sector and industry could provide opportunities to access a greater quantity of data than is possible for national governments alone due to financial constraints. This expanded level of communication could aid the implementation of the procedural obligations contained in IWL, including obligations to cooperate and to exchange data and information.[165] As stated by Leb, and as previously noted, the 'main difficulty for any riparian state planning a use is to come by all the information and data required to do a detailed assessment according to the equitable and reasonable use principle. The information needs are wide ranging and not all information is available at the national level'.[166] The WEF nexus could offer therefore not only tangible substantive findings on divergent water uses, but also facilitate information exchange, cooperation and the potential of taking joint action to maximise mutual benefits or avert potential risks through the identification of, and acting upon, trade-offs. The obvious weakness of the WEF nexus in the context of the duty at hand is that it does not have a binding force unless studies are solicited as part of a legal commitment between concerned states. However, the fact that nexus outcomes involve scholars or independent bodies means that the parties are likely to positively react to them and enhance their cooperative endeavour. In contrast to the WEF nexus, the SDGs have directly embraced relevant policy commitments to cooperation, supported by indicators for their implementation.

Further, the SDGs could be used by states to add substance to agreements for the joint management of watercourses, thereby enhancing cooperation. Successful transboundary water management is extremely dependant

163 Spijkers, *supra* note 24; O. McIntyre, '*International Water Law and SDG 6: Mutually Reinforcing Paradigms*', in D. French & L. J. Kotzé (Eds.), *Sustainable Development Goals: Law, Theory and Implementation* (Cheltenham: Edward Elgar, 2018) 173–200.

164 Hoff, *supra* note 91, at 225. See also Benson, Gain & Rouillard, *supra* note 22, at 760.

165 UNWC, *supra* note 2, Arts 8, 9.

166 C. Leb, '*Data Innovations for Transboundary Freshwater Resources Management: Are Obligations Related to Information Exchange Still Needed?*', 4.4, Brill Research Perspectives in International Water Law (2020) 3, 21.

on political buy-in and the commitment of states to cooperate.[167] Creating linkages across sectors, increasing participation and promoting information sharing across WEF sectors may improve the willingness of states to cooperate. As noted by McIntyre, 'the inclusive and participatory process' of the SDGs as well as the use of their implementation, monitoring and compliance mechanisms can be used to 'enhance the relevance and legitimacy of progressive water law'.[168]

In sum, it is clear that the LNG approach brings a holistic and innovating approach to water governance by strengthening substantive and procedural rules of IWL. While the application of this approach will differ on a case-by-case basis, the key linkages made remain relevant. The following section will broadly demonstrate how the approach may operate within one example, in this case, the ZRB.

4 The Zambezi River: LNG Approach

The ZRB spans eight countries in Southern Africa: Angola, Botswana, Malawi, Mozambique, Namibia, Tanzania, Zambia and Zimbabwe. It is the largest river basin contained within the Southern African Development Community (SADC), covering a total area of 1.37 million km^2. Each of the countries share different proportions of the basin and rely on it to different extents.[169] The basin comprises almost all of Malawi's territory, 76.4% of Zambia, 54.5% of Zimbabwe, 20.2% of Mozambique and 18.9% of Angola.[170] Each of the basin countries have diverse natural physical characteristics that create governance challenges, but also opportunities, particularly for economic development such as hydropower plants and agriculture that support food and energy security.[171] The ZRB is home to around 30 million people, 25% of whom live in

167 M. Lim, '*Is Water Different from Biodiversity? Governance Criteria for the Effective Management of Transboundary Resources*', 23:1, Review of European, Comparative and International Environmental Law (2014) 96–110, 99.

168 McIntyre, '*International Water Law and SDG 6*', *supra* note 163, at 174.

169 The World Bank, *The Zambezi River Basin: A Multi-Sector Investment Opportunities Analysis, Volume 4: Summary Report* (Washington, DC: The World Bank, 2010).

170 See Food and Agriculture Organization of the United Nations (FAO), '*The Zambezi Basin*', in *Irrigation Potential in Africa: A Basin Approach*, FAO Land and Water Bulletin 4 (Rome: FAO, 1997), http://www.fao.org/3/W4347E/w4347e00.htm#the%20zambezi%20basin, accessed 10 June 2019.

171 Significant hydropower facilities are serviced by the Zambezi River and its tributaries, including the joint Zambia and Zimbabwe Kariba dam (built in 1959), the Itezhi Tezhi

urban centres and the rest within rural areas.[172] Poverty continues to impact all of the ZRB states to varying degrees.[173] As a result a fine balance must be struck across the basin between the use of natural resources for economic growth, the implementation of international and regional legal obligations, and the pursuit of sustainable development.

Water law and policy frameworks throughout the ZRB have largely been developed in line with IWL frameworks, the UNWC in particular.[174] This framework has created a strong foundation for the governance of the watercourse. Yet, some gaps remain, particularly with regard to demonstrating linkages between water, energy and food, wider considerations of sustainable development, and implementation of IWL principles at a national level.

4.1 *Interpreting and Implementing* IWL

Of the ZRB states, only Namibia has ratified the UNWC; however, Angola, Botswana, Malawi, Mozambique and Zambia voted in favour of adoption of the treaty (Tanzania and Zimbabwe were absent from the voting process).[175] Therefore the UNWC cannot by applied to the ZRB as a binding international treaty framework. But, as noted above, many of the main principles and rules codified in the UNWC are reflected in customary law and are therefore applicable to all states. The key norms and procedures of the UNWC have also been endorsed in regional and basin-wide legal instruments in the ZRB, as will be discussed below. There is therefore no need for further discussion of customary IWL for the purpose of this monograph. As the UNWC is a framework convention, it needs to be applied to specific international watercourses or basins through separate agreements or with necessary adjustments and details. For these reasons this monograph focuses on regional, basin-wide and national laws and policy instruments relating to the Zambezi.

---

dam in Zambia (built in 1977), the Kafue Gorge Upper hydroelectric scheme in Zambia (commissioned in 1979) and the Cahora Bassa dam in Mozambique (built in 1974).

172 The World Bank, *supra* note 169.

173 United Nations Development Programme (UNDP), *Human Development Report 2016: Human Development for Everyone* (New York: UNDP, 2016), http://hdr.undp.org/sites/default/files/2016_human_development_report.pdf, accessed 10 July 2019. The gross national income (GNI) per capita of the countries in the region ranges from US$14,663 (Botswana), US$9,770 (Namibia) to that of US$1,588 (Zimbabwe), US$1,098 (Mozambique) and US$2,467 (Tanzania).

174 The UNWC is mentioned within regional and basin level frameworks, see SADC Revised Protocol, *supra* note 32, preamble; ZAMCOM Agreement, *supra* note 32, preamble.

175 UNGA, *Official Records*, 99th Plenary Meeting, 21 May 1997, UN Doc. A/51/PV.99.

4.1.1 Regional Frameworks

In the SADC,[176] to which all ZRB states belong, the first protocol concerning international watercourses was signed in 1995 and subsequently entered into force in 1998.[177] It was subsequently revised following the adoption of the UNWC and became the 2000 Revised Protocol on Shared Watercourses (SADC-PC or SADC Revised Protocol), bringing its basic principles in line with the developments in IWL, namely the UNWC.[178] The provisions of the SADC-PC largely replicate those of the UNWC, with a couple of alterations.[179] The factors relevant to equitable and reasonable use are identical to the UNWC, with the exception of Article 3(8)(a)(ii) which adds environmental needs of the watercourse state. In addition, within Article 4(2) the obligation not to cause significant harm is applied to both other watercourse states (as per the UNWC) and their environment, going further than the UNWC in relation to environmental needs. In addition to the Protocol, there have been several policy documents framing the implementation of regional water sector development.[180] In terms of ratification of the SADC-PC, all ZRB states have ratified the agreement, with the exception of Zimbabwe and Angola, which have only signed the agreement. The SADC-PC is well acknowledged as a leading regional framework for water governance, however, the extent to which the Protocol interacts with other sectors is limited. The factors used to determine equitable and reasonable use,

---

176 Law over transboundary watercourses in Southern Africa has been established through SADC, a political and economic intergovernmental organization formally established by the 1992 Treaty of the SADC. The goal of SADC is to further socio-economic, political and security cooperation and integration among the 15 Southern African state parties, with specific objectives to 'achieve complementarity between national and regional strategies and programmes', as well as to 'achieve sustainable utilisation of natural resources and effective protection of the environment'. Thus, while cooperation is the key goal of the SADC, environmental and natural resource issues are key components of such cooperation.

177 Ten SADC countries signed the agreement; Angola was still impacted by civil war at the time. See S. M. A. Salman, '*Legal Regime for Use and Protection of International Watercourses in the Southern African Region: Evolution and Context*', 41, Natural Resources Journal (2001) 981–1022.

178 SADC Revised Protocol, *supra* note 32.

179 See UN Watercourses Convention, 'UN Watercourses Convention and the SADC Revised Protocol', User's Guide Fact Sheet Series No. 13, https://www.unwatercoursesconvention.org/documents/UNWC-Fact-Sheet-13-Relationship-with-SADC-Revised-Protocol.pdf, accessed 12 April 2020.

180 Southern African Development Community Regional Water Policy (adopted August 2005); Southern African Development Community (adopted June 2006); Southern African Development Community Regional Infrastructure Development Master Plan, Water Sector Plan (adopted August 2012); Southern African Development Community Regional Strategic Action Plan on Integrated Water Resources Development and Management Phase IV (2016–2020).

contained in Article 8, mirror those of the UNWC. The same is true of the duty not to cause significant harm contained in Article 10. Thus, the SADC-PC, like the UNWC, largely creates a framework convention that can be adapted to fit the circumstances of individual watercourses.

4.1.2 Basin Frameworks

For cooperation to be successful at the basin level there must be a degree of established trust, confidence and information sharing between all of the relevant states. A long history of cooperation exists within the ZRB, and developments towards the joint management of water resources at the basin scale have been significant. This monograph will focus on the most recent period of transboundary water cooperation, beginning with the formation of the Zambezi River Authority (ZRA).[181]

In the aftermath of World War II, the territorial governments of Northern and Southern Rhodesia established the Inter-Territorial Hydroelectric Power Commission in order to research means of ending power outages.[182] The Commission looked into the potential of establishing two dams, the Kariba and the Kafue. The Kariba dam was subsequently built and became operational in 1959 under the jurisdiction of the Federal Power Board, and subsequently the Central African Power Corporation in 1963 and the ZRA in 1987. The main objective of the ZRA is to be responsible for 'the operation and maintenance of the Kariba Dam Complex, investigation and development of new dam sites on the Zambezi River and analysing and disseminating hydrological and environmental information pertaining to the Zambezi River and Lake Kariba'.[183] This is of significant importance within this monograph as it makes clear the importance of the WEF nexus from the very beginning of cooperation within the ZRB.

---

181 Early agreements were formed in the imperial era and largely focused on the demarcation of national boundaries, put in place by colonial governments, while agreements that came slightly later were largely bilateral. These agreements are nonetheless important as they acknowledge the history of cooperation within the basin. For a full analysis of all of the agreements formed within the ZRB, see D. Saruchera, J. Lautze, J. Mwale et al., '*Transboundary Water Cooperation: Taking Stock and Looking Forward*', in J. Lautze, Z. Phiri, V. Smakhtin & D. Saurchera (Eds.), *The Zambezi River Basin: Water and Sustainable Development* (Abingdon: Routledge, 2017) 175–192.

182 Soils Incorporated (Pvt) Ltd and Chalo Environmental and Sustainable Development Consultants, *Kariba Dam Case Study: Zambia and Zimbabwe Final Report*, prepared for the World Commission on Dams, Cape Town (2000), https://cpb-us-e1.wpmucdn.com/share.nanjing-school.com/dist/1/43/files/2013/05/World_Commission_on_Dams_2000_Case_Study_Kariba_Dam_Final_Report_November_2000-2etc5lv.pdf, accessed 10 June 2019.

183 Zambezi Water Authority, 'About Us', http://www.zambezira.org/about-us, accessed 10 June 2019.

The ZRA Agreement establishes the ZRA and charges it with the duty to 'operate, monitor and maintain the Kariba Complex'.[184] The ZRA Agreement entered into force on 1 October 1987 as a bilateral treaty between Zambia and Zimbabwe. Notably, while it is not a basin-wide agreement, it calls for efficient and equitable use of the waters of the Zambezi River.[185] It also states that all energy produced from the Kariba dam should be shared equally[186] and provides further details regarding equal water allocation in Annexure 1.[187] The Agreement also provides a number of cooperation and consultation obligations in Article 18(1) that are well developed for the time of its formation. Annexure 1 calls for the exchange of information that is 'of common interest related to the interconnected systems' (Article 22). It lists a number of obligations regarding consultations over planned measures and abstractions on the watercourse (Article 9(e) and 18), as well as cooperation over regulation of the water level and maintenance of hydraulic works and installations (Articles 9 and 22). Importantly a joint technical committee is established through Annexure 1[188] and obligations regarding dispute settlement are also put in place.[189] It has to be stressed here that the key principles within the ZRA Agreement are compatible with equitable and reasonable utilization and the principles of IWL. However, this Agreement went beyond equity by advocating the notion of 'perfect' equality of the sharing of benefits between the two parties.

Currently, the main legal framework within the ZRB is the ZAMCOM Agreement, an institutional agreement which specifically establishes the Zambezi Watercourse Commission (ZAMCOM).[190] The ZAMCOM Agreement is legally binding on all states that have ratified it, which currently includes all ZRB states with the exception of Malawi which has only signed the agreement. ZAMCOM states that its objective is 'to promote the equitable and reasonable utilisation of the water resources of the Zambezi Watercourse as well as the efficient management and sustainable development thereof'.[191] It's overall

184 Agreement between the Republic of Zimbabwe and the Republic of Zambia concerning the utilization of the Zambezi River (signed at Harare, 28 July 1987), Art. 9.

185 *Id.*, Art. 18(1).

186 *Id.*, Art. 23.

187 *Id.*

188 *Id.*, Art. 22.

189 *Id.*, Art. 32.

190 For a discussion on the need for greater clarity on the definition of river basin commissions and organisations, see S. Schmeier, A. K. Gerlak & S. Blumstein, '*Clearing the Muddy Waters of Shared Watercourses Governance: Conceptualizing International River Basin Organizations*', 16, International Environmental Agreements: Politics, Law and Economics (2106) 597–619.

191 See Zambezi Watercourse Commission, 'About ZAMCOM', http://www.zambezicommission.org/about-zamcom/about-zamcom, accessed 12 April 2019.

vision links to regional strategies developed at the SADC level, as well as various plans and policies adopted at basin level to envisage 'a future characterised by equitable and sustainable utilisation of water for social and environmental justice, regional integration and economic benefit for present and future generations'.[192] Therefore, even from the overall objective and vision, clear references to equitable and reasonable utilization derived from IWL and sustainable development can be seen.

ZAMCOM contains many of the key principles contained in the UNWC; Articles 12(1)(h) and 13 cover equitable and reasonable utilization of the watercourse, with factors relevant to equitable and reasonable use covered in Article 13(2). The obligation to prevent significant harm to other watercourse states is provided in Articles 12(1)(v) and 14(2), which seek to prevent, eliminate, mitigate or control adverse transboundary impacts (Article 14(3)). The Agreement also provides full cooperation and support to the Council and Technical Committee of ZAMCOM (Article 14(5)). In terms of the procedural framework, the Agreement establishes a joint institutional framework in Articles 3 to 9. It also promotes the regular exchange of available or obtainable data and information 'with regard to all aspects of the Zambezi Watercourse' (Article 15). Procedures regarding the exchange of information on planned measures and notification concerning planned measures with possible adverse effects are included in Article 16. Dispute settlement measures are also included within the Agreement in Article 16(5), 21 and 22. Importantly, a provision is also included regarding the harmonization of development plans with the Zambezi Strategic Plan in Article 14(9).

However, given the controversy around, for example, the customary status of the duty to exchange data and information in IWL, its inclusion in the ZAMCOM Agreement in unambiguous terms is notable.[193] Furthermore, the law-making steps taken by ZAMCOM are significant due to their intention to make obligations clearer for member states. This can also be seen in the work of the Commission to draft further information on procedural rules to provide further clarity. In February 2016, the ZAMCOM Council approved a new set of 'Rule and Procedures for Sharing Information and Data'.[194] The Rules apply to the sharing of data and information that is relevant to the 'equitable and

192 *Id.*

193 C. Leb, '*General Obligation to Cooperate and Regular Exchange of Data and Information (Articles 8 and 9)*', in Boisson de Chazournes et al., *supra* note 2, 134.

194 Zambezi Watercourse Commission, 'Rules and Procedures for Sharing of Data and Information Related to the Management and Development of the Zambezi Watercourse', adopted by the ZAMCOM Council, 25 February 2016, effective 26 March 2016, http://www.zambezicommission.org/sites/default/files/clusters_pdfs/16.07.28-Rules_

reasonable utilisation, management and sustainable development of the Zambezi Watercourse'.[195] Therefore, at the outset of the Rules, a clear link to the principles of IWL and to the notion of 'sustainable development' is made. The Rules and Procedures consist of two components: rules that apply to cost sharing and the roles of institutions, and the technical procedures and specifications identifying the data to be shared and the procedures which should be used to do so. Adopted in February 2017, the 'Procedures for Notification of Planned Measures' aims to provide member states with detailed 'notification requirements' including timelines, formats and supporting documents. In the same vein as the Procedures and Rules on sharing of information described above, the document begins by demonstrating a clear link to IWL, as well as linkages to both Article 16 of the ZAMCOM Agreement and Article 4 of the Revised SADC Protocol on Shared Watercourses.

ZAMCOM has also led to the establishment of basin-wide implementation plans, such as the 2008 Integrated Water Resources Management (IWRM) Strategy and Implementation Plan.[196] The Plan makes reference to all uses of water resources, including agriculture and hydropower and possible plans for expansion. The IWRM Plan notes the Southern African Power Pool (SAPP)[197] expansion plan up to 2025, which envisages development of several new power plants.[198] With regard to irrigation for agriculture, the Plan envisages a 'modest' expansion of 50%. It notes that although '[p]rima facie there are ample water resources in the basin' water availability needs to be assessed in terms of drought years as well as the impact on existing water uses.[199] However, while there is brief mention of a number of international legal frameworks and the SADC Revised Protocol, there is no mention of the UNWC (although the Convention was not yet in force at the time). There is also little to relate the legal obligations to the Plan.

ProceduresForDataSharing_Adopted-by-Council_FinalEditing_Ver10_FINAL.pdf, accessed 10 September 2019.

195 *Id.*, Art. 2.

196 Integrated Water Resources Management (IWRM) Strategy and the Implementation Plan for the Zambezi River Basin, April 2008, http://www.zambezicommission.org/sites/default/files/clusters_pdfs/Zambezi%20River_Basin_IWRM_Strategy_ZAMSTRAT.pdf, accessed 9 June 2019.

197 The SADC region formed the Southern African Power Pool (SAPP) in 1995, based on the Protocol on Energy, to strengthen regional cooperation and growth through energy resources. See SADC Protocol on Energy (signed 24 August 1996, entered into force 17 April 1998); Southern African Power Pool, 'About Us', http://www.sapp.co.zw/about-sapp, accessed 10 February 2020.

198 IWRM Strategy and Implementation Plan, *supra* note 196.

199 *Id.*, at 26.

Therefore, at the basin scale, elaborate and comprehensive frameworks are in place through ZAMCOM. Significant progress has been made within the basin to form joint cooperative frameworks and establish mechanisms for data and information sharing. However, legal commitments are often lost within the scope of strategy and policy documents and one clear cohesive framework is not easily identified. While plans relating to IWRM demonstrate understanding of the importance of taking a holistic approach, there is little information regarding how this will be implemented. Better integration across such strategy and policy documents, linked to IWL commitments, but through the frame of the LNG approach could allow the ZRB to streamline targets to increase efficiency and sustainability as elaborated next.

4.2 *WEF Nexus*

Each aspect of the WEF nexus can be easily demonstrated within the ZRB. The basin has an estimated 20,000 MW of hydropower potential;[200] however, to date, only around 5,000 MW of this potential has been exploited.[201] As a result, there is great interest in the Zambezi's hydroelectric potential from international development agencies, international funders and each of the riparian states, as well as countries just outside of the ZRB, such as South Africa.[202] Although hydropower is a non-consumptive activity, it still accounts for the largest share of water use within the basin through loss in evaporation.[203] More than 30 large dams have been built on the Zambezi, including Mozambique's Cahora Bassa dam and the Kariba dam between

---

200 M. Tumbare, 'The Zambezi River: Its Threats and Opportunities', presented at The Zambezi River: It's Threats and Opportunities, 7th River Symposium, 1–3 September 2004, Brisbane, Australia, http://archive.riversymposium.com/2004/index.php?element=Tumbare+M, accessed 12 April 2020.

201 A. Tilmant, *'Hydropower and the Water-Energy-Food Nexus'*, in J. Lautze, Z. Phiri, V. Smakhtin & D. Saurchera (Eds.), *The Zambezi River Basin: Water and Sustainable Development* (Abingdon: Routledge, 2017) 82–101, 86.

202 See The World Bank, 'Zambezi River Basin Development Project', http://projects.worldbank.org/P133380?lang=en, accessed 9 June 2019. Further, under the African Union, the New Partnership for Africa's Development (NEPAD) runs the Programme for Infrastructure Development in Africa (PIDA), which contributes to the development of regional and continental infrastructure in energy and other sectors up to 2030, with a broad scope that includes transboundary water resources. See African Development Bank Group, 'Programme for Infrastructure Development in Africa (PIDA)', https://www.afdb.org/en/topics-and-sectors/initiatives-partnerships/programme-for-infrastructure-development-in-africa-pida/, accessed 9 June 2019.

203 See X. Cai, Y. Altchenko & G. Chavula, *'Availability and use of water resources'*, in J. Lautze, Z. Phiri, V. Smakhtin & D. Saurchera (Eds.), *The Zambezi River Basin: Water and Sustainable Development* (Abingdon: Routledge, 2017) 7–28, 19.

Zambia and Zimbabwe. These dams provide the majority of the basin's hydropower,[204] and therefore also contribute the lion's share of total evaporation, with the Cahora Bassa accounting for around 35% and the Kariba accounting for more than half. All of the ZRB states depend on hydroelectricity from the ZRB as a major energy source for industry.[205]

With regard to food, the ZRB is a major contributor to food security in the region, primarily due to its role in sustaining agricultural activities and fisheries. Around 5.2 million hectares are cultivated annually in the basin, and 85% of this area sits within Zimbabwe, Zambia and Malawi.[206] Agriculture is mostly rain-fed or flood dependant. Subsistence agriculture is practiced by the majority of the rural population in the basin, along flood plains, swamps, wetlands and at the edges of large water bodies. The river system is therefore vital in maintaining the ecosystem that ensures the seasonal fluctuations sustaining agriculture. While livestock accounts for 0.11% of water use in the basin, irrigated agriculture accounts for 1.43%. Given that much of the agricultural practices in the ZRB are rain-fed, the increased erratic, unreliable rainfall with frequent multiyear low rainfall cycles brought about by climate change present a huge challenge to agricultural practices in the basin.[207] In addition, water pollution and unregulated water use, including storage for hydropower generation, threatens the flood plain areas that are important for agriculture, while flood control requires careful cooperation with regard to reservoir operations. This is strong evidence of the tension between water use for energy on the one hand, and for food production on the other hand. There is also an opportunity to use energy production to provide a widely regulated water flow, which might help to mitigate flooding and provide a more predictable flow of water to be used for agricultural activities.[208]

204 The World Bank *supra* note 169.

205 *Id.*

206 IWRM Strategy and Implementation Plan, *supra* note 196.

207 The World Bank, *supra* note 169.

208 These challenges are also relevant to fisheries in the ZRB, which are critically dependent upon sufficient quantities of water of specific quality to support the aquatic ecosystem and access to breeding areas. These factors have been disrupted by large developments and water abstraction, which have affected flow regimes, water chemistry, sediment load and temperature. For example, the construction of the Kafue dams led to a decline in fish production, fish biodiversity and flood plain pasture, and the Cahora Bassa dam has led to there being little seasonal variation in river flow at Tete and unpredictable flooding. The resulting change in fisheries across the basin has had economic damage and lead to concerns regarding environmental flow requirements to support ecosystems and biodiversity.

Water is an essential human need, however, domestic consumption, even with projected population growth in the Zambezi Basin, makes up a very small percentage of use.[209] Despite the huge quantities of water within the ZRB, many in the region still lack adequate access to clean water and sanitation.[210] A number of water transfer schemes are used throughout the basin to transport water to urban centres that are vulnerable to drought. Tensions between riparian's have occurred previously over such plans, for example, Zimbabwe's Matabeleland Zambezi Water Project, which aims to pipe water from the Zambezi to the city of Bulawayo, threatening water supply to Mozambique.[211] South Africa has also expressed interest in large water diversion projects from the Zambezi at Kazungula through Botswana to Pretoria.[212]

Therefore, WEF nexus issues within the ZRB are easily identifiable, illustrated through a bounty of benefits that can be derived from the watercourse. While several developments have already taken place across the ZRB, both in relation to hydropower and irrigation schemes, huge potential remains. The importance of the WEF nexus within this region has never been greater; each future development will likely impact one aspect of the WEF nexus, and appropriate steps must be taken to ensure that the integrity of the water resource is retained while developmental goals are pursued.

Support for the implementation of a WEF nexus approach can be illustrated at a regional level in the SADC through a number of policy documents and strategies. The SADC Regional Water Policy was adopted in 2005[213] and is implemented through the Regional Strategy Action Plan (RESAP); the current

---

209 See X. Cai, Y. Altchenko & G. Chavula, '*Availability and use of water resources*', in J. Lautze et al., *supra* note 203, at 19.

210 See JMP, World Health Organisation & UNICEF 'Hygiene Baselines pre-COVID-19 Global Snapshot' (2020), https://washdata.org/sites/default/files/documents/reports/2020-05/JMP-2020-COVID-global-hygiene-snapshot.pdf, accessed 30 July 2020. For instance, the report notes that in Zambia the percentage of households with basic water is 60%, while the percentage with basic hygiene falls to 14%.

211 A. Swain, '*Politics or Development: Sharing of International Rivers in the South*', in J. Öjendal, S. Hansson & S. Hellberg (Eds.), *Politics and Development in a Transboundary Watershed: The Case of the Lower Mekong Basin* (Dordrecht: Springer, 2012) 19–35, 29.

212 *Id.*

213 SADC, *Regional Water Policy* (August 2005), https://www.sadc.int/files/1913/5292/8376/Regional_Water_Policy.pdf, accessed 15 June 2019. Support for an integrated approach to water governance can also be seen in the IWRM Strategy and Implementation Plan for the Zambezi Basin. See Zambezi Watercourse Commission, *Integrated Water Resources Management Strategy and Implementation Plan for the Zambezi River Basin: At a Glance* (Harare: ZAMCOM, 2016). http://www.zambezicommission.org/publication/integrated-water-resources-management-strategy-and-implementation-plan-zambezi-river-0, accessed 4 April 2019.

iteration of RESAP (2015–2020) is made up of eight programmes, one of which is the WEF nexus. Further, the SADC WEF Nexus Operational Framework is currently being developed[214] to provide guidance and tools to make decisions, coordinate between different sectors and facilitate nexus investments in the SADC region. It can be assumed that this framework will be utilized in order to guide implementation, as, currently, despite the presence of the WEF nexus action plan, there is little or no evidence of linkages across the sectors.[215]

In relation to energy, the SADC has a Regional Energy Access Strategy Action Plan which was approved in 2011 and sets broad goals for improving access to modern forms of energy as well as specific policy mechanisms to achieve increased access.[216] This is in addition to the previously mentioned SAPP, which demonstrates the desire for coordination within the region.[217] The 2004 Dar-es-Salaam Declaration on Agriculture and Food Security in the SADC Region was signed with the aim of improving water management and irrigation by encouraging member states to allocate a portion of agricultural budgets to water management and irrigation development.[218] Subsequently, the Regional Agricultural Policy (RAP) was adopted in 2014 and implemented through the Regional Agricultural Investment Plan (RAIP), which was adopted in March 2017, the RAP discusses integrated approaches on water resources and highlights the importance of water for meeting food security, stressing that scarcity of water resources and increased competition for water across multiple sectors will reduce water availability for agriculture.[219]

---

214 GWP, 'SADC convenes workshop to validate the WEF Nexus Framework and test the Nexus Tool' (16 September 2019), https://www.gwp.org/en/GWP-SouthernAfrica/About-GWP-SAF/more/News/sadc-convenes-workshop-to-validate-the-wef-nexus-framework-and-test-the-nexus-tool/, accessed 30 July 2020. It is unclear whether the framework has been finalised as of 31 July 2020.

215 SADC is also a partner in the Nexus Regional Dialogues Programme, with an aim to create an enabling environment to drive cross-sectoral engagement and implementation of nexus investment projects. See Nexus, 'Nexus: Management Experience for Water, Energy and Food Security', https://www.nexus-dialogue-programme.eu, accessed 15 April 2020.

216 SADC, 'SADC Regional Energy Access Strategy and Action Plan' (March 2010), http://www.euei-pdf.org/en/sadc-regional-energy-access-strategy-and-action-plan, accessed 20 April 2019.

217 SAPP, 'About SAPP', http://www.sapp.co.zw/about-sapp, accessed 10 February 2020.

218 See Dar-es-Salaam Declaration on Agriculture and Food Security in the SADC Region, signed 15 May 2004, https://www.resakss.org/sites/default/files/SADC%202004%20Dar-es-Salaam%20Declaration%20on%20Agriculture%20and%20Food%20Security.pdf, accessed 10 May 2020, Art. 5.

219 SADC, *Regional Agricultural Policy* (August 2014), https://www.nepad.org/publication/sadc-regional-agricultural-policy-0, accessed 20 April 2019, Section 10.5.

Significant investment and commitment at the regional level is demonstratable within each WEF sector independently, and across the WEF nexus as a whole, illustrating a drive to integrate the governance of the three sectors. This commitment can also be seen though the joint meetings that have taken place between the SADC Ministries on Water and Energy annually since 2016.[220] While ambitions to implement a WEF nexus approach are clear within the ZRB, use of the SDGs at a basin level is less clear.

4.3 *The Sustainable Development Goals*

As will be discussed in the following section, commitment to the SDGs is illustrated within the National Development Plans (NDPs) of many of ZRB states. Further, there are several references to sustainable development and intergenerational equity across the national laws of the ZRB.[221] As discussed above, the long history of cooperation within the ZRB will go a long way to the achievement of SDG 6. For instance, with regard to target 6.5, ZAMCOM already is able to assess the operational success of the Integrated Water Resources Management Strategy, demonstrating the alignment of the basin with the SDGs. This established framework can then be improved and strengthened, subject to continuous review. The first period of reporting on the progress of indicator 6.5.2 demonstrated strong operational arrangements were in place in relation to the SADC, where over 70% of transboundary river and lake basins are covered by operational arrangements.[222]

However, more could be done to explicitly demonstrate the interlinkages across the SDGs, increasing focus on the achievement of SDGs 2 (food) and 7 (energy), as well as SDG 6 (water). As has previously been stated, the achievement of each of the SDGs will have a strong dependence on water resources: as

220 SADC, 'Statement: SADC Joint Meeting of Ministers of Energy and for Water held in Windhoek, Namibia on 24th May 2019', https://www.sadc.int/files/1615/5895/0326/Statement_-_Wate_and_Energy_24May_2019_final.pdf, accessed 10 May 2020.

221 Angola: 1998 Environmental Law No. 5/98; Malawi: 2013 Water Management Act (No. 2 of 2013), Art 2, 104; 2001 Irrigation Act (No. 16 of 2001); Mozambique: 1997 Act No. 20/97 approving the Environment Act; Namibia: 2013 Water Resources Management Act (No. 11 of 2013), Art. 3(d); 2007 Environmental Management Act (No. 7 of 2007), Arts 1, 3(2)(f); Tanzania: 2009 Water Resources Management Act (No. 11 of 2009), Art. 5; 2005 Environmental Impact Assessment and Audit Regulations, (G.N. No. 349 of 2005), Art. 45(a); Zambia: 2011 Water Resources Management Act (No. 21 of 2011), Art. 2; 2011 Environmental Management Act (No. 12 of 2011), Art. 2; Zimbabwe: 2002 Environmental Management Agency Act [Chapter 20:27], Art. 4(2)(e).

222 United Nations and UNESCO (on behalf of UN-Water), *Progress on Transboundary Water Cooperation: Global baseline for SDG indicator 6.5.2* (Paris: UNESCO, 2018), https://www.unwater.org/publications/progress-on-transboundary-water-cooperation-652/, accessed 10 May 2020, at 36.

such, clear and focused evaluation of the needs and uses of the resources must be made, utilizing both the WEF nexus and the framework of IWL. ZAMCOM is also in a unique position to be able to take a holistic overview of the basin and its resources, identifying the best means of benefit sharing to ensure resources are used in the most sustainable and equitable way across the basin countries. For this reason, it is essential that monitoring is conducted at basin level ensuring that such decisions are evidence-based and data-driven, enhancing policymaking.

As it currently stands, the regional and basin approaches applicable to the ZRB are strong, at least on paper. There is, however, little evidence of the extent to which the various plans and policy frameworks are implemented; and in particular, the extent to which they are implemented uniformly across the basin. The plethora of documents, plans and strategies risks the focus of ZAMCOM being split across the achievement of too many targets, limiting capacity and leading to poor utilization of resources. Adopting the LNG approach, with a focus on IWL at the core, substantiated by the WEF nexus and driving towards the SDG targets and indicators may provide a more streamlined approach to the governance of the basin. Of course, the operationalization of such an approach will be further aided by ensuring a degree of consistency across each of the basin states. Therefore, the following section will provide a snapshot of the existing frameworks within each ZRB country.

4.4 *National Strategies: LNG Perspective*

In order for IWL to be implemented successfully, national principles of water governance must be generally consistent, if not identical, across basin states.[223] At the national level in the ZRB, there is a lack of consistent domestication of key principles of IWL. It is not within the scope of this monograph to provide an overview of the implementation of each of the principles of IWL at the national level, therefore only a brief discussion of key principles and rules will be considered. NDPs, policies and legal frameworks have also been reviewed for the purpose of understanding not only the legal commitments made by each state, but also future and more aspirational agendas that are often contained within policy and development frameworks, which allow for greater articulation and ultimate implementation of the LNG approach.[224]

---

223 For discussion of the need to give due regard to the asymmetry between countries on watercourses, see P. Van der Zaag, '*Asymmetry and Equity in Water Resources Management Critical Institutional Issues for Southern Africa*', 21:12, Water Resources Management (2007) 1993–2004.

224 It should be noted that due to language constraints, it has not been possible to conduct a comprehensive analysis of the legal and policy frameworks of Angola. While similar

4.4.1 Angola

As previously noted, Angola has not formally ratified the UNWC, but has signed the SADC Revised Protocol and ratified the ZAMCOM Agreement, both of which incorporate the core principles of IWL. Some of these principles have also been domesticated through the National Water Law (Act No. 6 of 2002).[225] Article 19(1b) provides for the 'fair and reasonable assignment of waters of common interest or joint interest thereof, in accordance with the interests and obligations assumed in the republic of Angola'. Although the provision does not contain explicit reference to equitable and reasonable use, the use of 'fair and reasonable' demonstrates some intention to manage shared watercourses in a manner which is equitable. Decree 82 also notes that water must be used efficiently, although no further detail is provided as to the meaning of the phrase or how it might be determined.[226] Significantly, the principle of equitable and reasonable use is included within some of the bilateral agreements that Angola is party to. The CUVECOM Agreement[227] between Angola and Namibia contains a provision on equitable and reasonable use in Article 4(1). The obligation not to cause significant harm is also included within bi- and multilateral agreements, as well as legislation relating to environmental impact assessments (EIAs), but not within legislation that relates to water directly.[228] Article 11(3) of CUVECOM states that countries should take all appropriate measures to prevent 'significant harm'. There are no provisions on notification for planned developments within the water law of Angola.

Angola included little information in the progress report submitted for SDG indicator 6.5.2. However, the main challenge cited was 'lack of human and financial resources and lack of effective institutions at river basin level'.[229]

---

difficulties were found with regard to Mozambique, enough information could be gathered from translated documents.

225 Government of Angola, Lei no. 6/02 [Law on Water Use, No. 6 of 2002], 21 June 2002, http://extwprlegs1.fao.org/docs/pdf/ang63753.pdf, accessed 10 April 2020.

226 *Id.*, Art. 10(1).

227 Agreement between the Government of the Republic of Angola and The Government of the Republic of Namibia on the Establishment of Cuvelai Watercourse Commission (9), 16 September 2014.

228 ENSafrica & One World Group, *Equivalence Assessment of National Water Laws among Riparian States in the Zambezi River Basin: ZAMCOM Agreement Comparative Assessment & Gap Analysis* (11 September 2017), https://oneworldgroup.co.za/wp-content/uploads/2019/06/20171020-ZCOM-D4-Revised-.pdf last accessed July 2019, accessed 3 February 2020, at 105.

229 UNECE, 'Reporting under SDG Indicator 6.5.2: Angola Country Report' (19 June 2017), https://www.unece.org/fileadmin/DAM/env/water/activities/Reporting_convention/All_countries/ANGOLA_Reporting_SDG652_final_19.06.2017.pdf, accessed 12 April 2020.

Angola cited as its main achievement the establishment of the Joint River Basin Commission, the establishment of Permanent Secretariats for river basin commissions, the design of basin-wide strategic plans, political will, good neighbourliness and a common vision among riparian countries.[230]

Little information could be found regarding any use of a WEF nexus approach within Angola. However, it is recognized that this is likely a limitation resulting from language constraints and may not be representative of the use of the framework within the country. Based on the information that could be sourced, it is still possible to make a preliminary observation that the problem of human and financial capacity may be aided by creating a more streamlined approach, such as the LNG approach. The fact that Angola reported on indicator 6.5.2 should be viewed positively as evidence of its willingness to work towards the achievement of the SDGs and to engage in transboundary cooperation.

4.4.2 Botswana

Legislation covering water resources in Botswana is no longer in line with more recent ambitions as expressed within the Draft Water Bill or the National Water Policy. The Water Act of 1969, the Water Works Act 1969, the Water Utilities Corporation Act 1970 and the Borehole Act 1956 represent a different era of water resources governance. Therefore, in 2005 a Draft Water Bill was formed to give a much-needed update to the existing legal framework. The 2005 Draft Water Bill for Botswana refers to the promotion of 'equitable and effective regional cooperation in the management of shared watercourse systems'.[231] It further states that the minister shall 'keep under review any bilateral and multilateral regional agreements for the purposes of promoting Botswana's interest in the mutual co-operation of states on shared waters on an equitable basis and in line with any developing international legal norms'.[232] The framework therefore makes progress towards the domestication of IWL principles. However, the draft has remained at the bill stage since 2005. The principle of no significant harm is also missing from the legal framework of water governance but is in place via EIA requirements.[233] With relation to international and regional instruments, Botswana has ratified both the SADC Revised Protocol and the ZAMCOM Agreement.

---

230 *Id.*

231 Government of Botswana, Draft Water Bill 2005, http://limpopo.riverawarenesskit.org/LIMPOPORAK_COM/_SYSTEM/DMSSTORAGE/3461EN/DRAFT_BOTSWANA_WATER_BILL_1.PDF, accessed 10 July 2019, Art. 55.

232 *Id.*

233 Government of Botswana, Environmental Assessment Act (No. 10 of 2011), Form E, Regulation 8.

In the absence of progress in legislation, the government has made some changes with policy frameworks, including the 1991 National Water Master Plan and 2006 review, the 2012 National Water Policy,[234] and the 2013 Integrated Water Resource Management Efficiency Plan 2013 (IWRM-EP).[235] The National Water Policy sets out a number of principles to guide water resources management, namely equity, sustainability and sufficiency. While equitable and reasonable use is not detailed as a fundamental objective of the Policy, 'equitable and reasonable use' between transboundary states is one of its aims. Significant harm is not discussed within the policy. Priority of use of water resources is given to meeting basic needs, in line with the UNWC, while the environment, agriculture and industry are subsequent priorities. There is no mention of how water allocation relating to each of these services links to transboundary needs. This omission is significant given that elsewhere the Botswanan policies and plans highlight transboundary issues and the importance of international agreements. For instance, Chapter 12 of the Water Policy is dedicated to international cooperation and contains several specific domestic strategies to facilitate international cooperation.

Included in such strategies are the strengthening of the institutional and policy framework to support an integrated approach to transboundary resources, consolidating and strengthening transboundary agreements, provisions of guidance for their management, benefit sharing, cooperation with riparian states in the development, use and protection of resources, implementing a comprehensive and compatible monitoring system for shared information, developing national systems to monitor obligations of international agreements, the promotion of joint planning and the use and protection of such resources, in addition to implementing best practice for stakeholder engagement. The inclusion of these provisions within the Water Policy are positive and largely in line with, if not the direct principles expressed in IWL, at least the overarching goals such as cooperation. However, their inclusion within a non-binding policy framework provides them with no legal authority as they exist within the remit of soft law.

Significantly, within the IWRM-EP Botswana also proposes the consideration of sector 'quotas' for irrigation and allocation of water resources, yet there are no legal provisions which would actually allow this. Nonetheless the inclusion is notable due to its alignment with the LNG approach developed within this

---

234 Government of Botswana, *Botswana National Water Policy* (October 2012), http://extwprlegs1.fao.org/docs/pdf/bot179129.pdf, accessed 10 July 2019.

235 Department of Water Affairs, Ministry of Minerals, Energy and Water Resources, *Botswana Integrated Water Resources Management & Water Efficiency Plan* (L. Kikobe, Ed.) (Gaborone: Government of Botswana, 2013), https://www.gwp.org/globalassets/global/activities/impact-stories/further-reading/iwrm-we-plan.pdf, accessed 10 July 2019.

monograph. Botswana is also one of few ZRB countries that mentions benefit sharing within its 2012 Water Policy.[236] No expansion of what this would involve is given, but the development of 'guidelines' to facilitate the benefit sharing is proposed. The IWRM-EP is also highlighted in Botswana's eleventh NDP (NDP11) which states that the Plan will promote 'the optimal utilisation of energy and water resources'.[237] NDP11 also mentions the importance of IWRM more generally and emphasizes the role that transboundary water resources play in Botswana's water security 'as the country will depend heavily on international waters'.[238] The NDP recognizes the scarcity of water resources and identifies water and energy as challenges for the agricultural sector, therefore recognizing the relationship between each aspect of the WEF nexus. It further states that 'for the SDGs to be realised, the projects to deliver Botswana's new vision and national priorities set out in NDP11 will be designed in a way which delivers the targets under each goal to the greatest extent possible'.[239]

In the report submitted relating to indicator 6.5.2 regarding the Zambezi, Botswana highlighted that one of the main difficulties it faced with implementing the frameworks in place is that the EIA processes for each member state are not well aligned with the Revised SADC Protocol. It is also stated that interpretation of certain clauses within basin agreements, such as ZAMCOM differ; in particular, equitable use is cited as a provision for which interpretation differs. As a strength, Botswana highlights the sharing of water in the Zambezi, emphasizing that conflict resolution processes work well. Botswana notes that there are no difficulties or challenges regarding data exchange, noting that the management of extreme events like floods and droughts are one of the main benefits from data exchange. One of the main achievements of joint monitoring described was frequent sharing of up-to-date information, while one of the main difficulties was limited funding for planned activities, capacity building and upgrading. With regard to joint assessments conducted by all the riparian states, Botswana highlights the ongoing development of a decision support system and the ZAMCOM strategic plan, which will be a 'master development plan comprising a general planning tool and process for the identification, categorisation and prioritization of project and programmes for the efficient management and sustainable development' of the Zambezi watercourse.

---

236 Botswana National Water Policy, *supra* note 234, Sections 12.1.6, 3.1.12.

237 Government of Botswana, *National Development Plan 11, Volume 1, April 2017–March 2023*, http://extwprlegs1.fao.org/docs/pdf/bot175398.pdf, accessed 10 May 2020, at 110.

238 *Id.*, at 134.

239 *Id.*, at 24.

In answering the question about the main challenges the country faces in cooperating on transboundary water, Botswana listed the lack of available data, the irregular attendance at scheduled meetings by other member states, and that the sovereignty of member states still seems to prevail, with limited clarity on the benefits of cooperation.[240] The main achievements of cooperation on transboundary waters were highlighted as the sharing of the waters, the sustenance of the basins ecosystems, economic benefits for member states and compliance with the SADC Protocol. Funding support gained from donor agencies was also noted as a positive. Under further comments, Botswana notes that it still requires funding to address the shortfall in water resources management. The report also highlighted that there needs to be increased capacity of riparian states to adopt a basin-wide approach to issues as there are still difficulties when trying to 'draw a line between national interests and basin interests'.[241]

What is clear from the policy framework in Botswana is that an LNG approach would be well placed to tie together existing goals. What is currently absent is a strong legal framework that could act as the backbone for such developments. When revising its legal framework, Botswana could draw upon the LNG approach to provide an intersectoral perspective to water allocation, as is desired in the IWRM-WE. In doing so, the legal framework could be in line with a WEF nexus approach and could link with the holistic strategy for implementing the SDGs, as is expressed in NDP11.

4.4.3 Malawi

Malawi has not ratified the UNWC but has ratified the SADC Revised Protocol and has signed the ZAMCOM Agreement. Water resources are regulated at a national level through the Water Resources Act No. 2 of 2013 (WRA). The WRA does not enact many of the principles of IWL, and in the instances where provisions relating to key principles are included, the language used does not denote positive obligations to take action, but rather is often framed within the language of steps which 'may' be taken if deemed appropriate. Reference to 'equitable, efficient and sustainable utilization' of watercourses in conformity with 'national legislation, and with regional and international water and

240 UNECE, 'Reporting under SDG Indicator 6.5.2: Botswana Country Report' (23 June 2017), https://www.unece.org/fileadmin/DAM/env/water/activities/Reporting_convention/All_countries/BOTSWANA_Reporting_SDG652_final_23.06.2017.pdf, accessed 12 April 2020.

241 *Id.*

environmental conventions' is, however, detailed under the obligations of catchment management committees in Article 33.[242]

A National Water Policy was developed in 2005, and the 2013 Water Resources Act notes that the National Water Policy aims to direct the way that water resources are managed, protected, used, developed, conserved and controlled.[243] The WRA states that the objectives and goals of water policy must be translated into practice when implementing the Act. It also provides for the development of a National Water Resources Master Plan, which was published in 2013 and provides a fairly comprehensive view of water management.[244] The National Water Policy details principles of IWL such as equitable, efficient and sustainable use.[245] There is, therefore, a gap between law and policy regarding the domestication of principles of IWL. Within the Master Plan, water allocation in relation to the WEF nexus is discussed, as is the water balance in relation to irrigation, while hydropower is noted as a feasible option. Yet, while the water actually required for hydropower is noted, there is no discussion of water availability as it relates to hydropower.

The Malawi Growth and Development Strategy (MGDS) (2017–2022) and Vision 2020 view water governance through the lens of a LNG approach.[246] The importance of the relationship between agriculture and water development is stated at the outset of the Strategy, which notes that 'efforts to improve agricultural productivity will not yet yield meaningful results unless water resources management and other related aspects are improved'.[247] The plan continues, 'increased investment in irrigation cannot succeed without addressing water conservation and catchment area, as well as ecosystems management'.[248] The MGDS also makes note of the importance of the SDGs, as well as making linkages to other international law and policy documents.[249] Despite being highlighted within the MGDS, a report relating to indicator 6.5.2 was

242 Government of Malawi, The Water Resources Act (No. 2 of 2013), http://extwprlegs1.fao.org/docs/pdf/mlw167598.pdf, accessed 10 August 2019, Part IV, Section 34(1).

243 *Id.*, Part IV, Section 34(1).

244 Government of Malawi, *National Water Resources Master Plan* (2013), https://openjicareport.jica.go.jp/pdf/12184537_07.pdf, accessed 12 April 2020.

245 Government of Malawi, *National Water Policy* (2005), https://cepa.rmportal.net/Library/government-publications/National%20Water%20Policy%202005.pdf/at_download/file, accessed 20 August 2019, Sections 2.0, 3.3.1, 4.1.5.

246 Government of Malawi, *The Malawi Growth and Development Strategy* (*MGDS*) *III* (*2017–2022*) (November 2017), https://www.undp.org/content/dam/malawi/docs/UNDP_Malawi_MGDS)%20III.pdf, accessed 20 August 2019.

247 *Id.*, at 16.

248 *Id.*

249 *Id.*, at 32.

not submitted by Malawi. The Strategy also specifically recognizes that it is 'imperative that national plans domesticate all the international, regional and continental frameworks for easy implementation, monitoring and reporting'.[250] The overall goal for agriculture, water development and climate change management is 'to achieve sustainable agricultural transformation and water development that is adaptive to climate change and enhances ecosystem services'.[251] The subsequent strategy for the realization of this goal clearly recognizes the WEF nexus, bringing together food security with IWRM.[252] The importance of energy is also recognized within the Strategy, although cross-cutting linkages with water and food are not provided. Within Vision 2020, increasing access to water is listed as an ambition, noting that current water supplies are from unreliable sources and run by inadequate institutional arrangements.[253]

Therefore, in a similar vein to Botswana, the policy framework of Malawi is more advanced than the legal framework. The goals of the MGDS and Vision 2020 are in harmony with the LNG approach. In the absence of a national legal framework that can act as the backbone of such developments, Malawi could look to IWL, as represented in the SADC-PC and the ZAMCOM Agreement, to provide a support mechanism for the advancement of water governance.

4.4.4 Mozambique

Like Angola, Mozambique also follows the approach that international law comes into force as soon as it is ratified and can be applied in national courts. Mozambique has not formally ratified the UNWC and has therefore not domesticated it into national water law; however, it has ratified the ZAMCOM Agreement and the SADC Protocol. The Water Law of 1991 is the primary framework for water governance and emphasizes the need for management of water on the basis of river basins, pricing and water allocation, as well as providing a decentralized system of governance. The Water Law states that international cooperation should aim to adopt coordinated measures for the management of watercourses within the same river basin, taking into account the interests

250 *Id.*, at 33.

251 *Id.*, at 57.

252 *Id.*, at 59.

253 Government of Malawi, *Vision 2020: The National Long-term Development Perspective for Malawi: A Summary* (Lilongwe: National Economic Council 2000), https://cepa.rmportal.net/Library/government-publications/Vision%202020-%20The%20National%20Long%20Term%20Development%20Perspective%20for%20Malawi.pdf/at_download/file, accessed 10 May 2020.

of all states concerned which demonstrates, even if indirectly, the spirit of equitable and reasonable use.[254]

Mozambique's Agenda 2025[255] emphasizes the importance of land, water and hydropower potential.[256] It also cites the enforcement of international and regional protocols and conventions, specifically those for sharing the water of international rivers, as providing opportunity for development.[257] Significantly, under the threats listed, it states that 'water and energy shortages may give rise to difficult relations between SADC States'.[258] This point is reiterated later in the document, where it is stated that it is 'foreseen that in forthcoming years water becomes one of the main sources of conflict between the countries in the region'. Agenda 2025 emphasizes the downstream position of Mozambique and the need for cooperation. No mention is made of the SDGs or the WEF nexus within the document and no report was submitted with regard to SDG 6.5.2.

Analysis relating to Mozambique has, in the same way as for Angola, been limited by language difficulties. However, what can be reasonably stated is that clearly each of the LNG components are important for the development of Mozambique's international watercourses and the structure for the adoption of an LNG approach in Mozambique does seem to be in place.

4.4.5 Namibia

At a regional and basin level, Namibia has ratified both the SADC Revised Protocol and the ZAMCOM Agreement. In 2004 Namibia brought into force the Water Resources Management Act (No. 24 of 2004) to replace the Water Act (No. 54 of 1956). The 1956 Act was based largely on private ownership of water and paid little regard to principle of equitable and reasonable use. While the 2004 Act should have made some headway in the legal framework, it was never brought into effect and was subsequently repealed and replaced by the 2013 Water Resources Management Act (No. 11 of 2013). The 2013 Act advocates the

254 Government of Mozambique, 1991 Act No. 16/91 regulating water resources belonging to the public domain. Mozambique also has in place a 1995 Water Policy; however, it was not possible to obtain or interpret it due to limitations in relation to the language barrier.

255 For an analysis of the different stages of water governance which have taken place in Mozambique, see R. Alba & A. Bolding, '*IWRM* Avant *la Lettre? Four Key Episodes in the Policy Articulation of IWRM in Downstream Mozambique*', 9 Water Alternatives (2016) 549–568.

256 Government of Mozambique, *Agenda 2025*, https://www.foresightfordevelopment.org/sobipro/55/130-agenda-2025-the-nations-vision-and-strategies, accessed 10 August 2019, at 59.

257 *Id.*, at 60.

258 *Id.*, at 61.

'furtherance of the objectives of the SADC Revised Protocol in Article 28(b), which includes the provision of equitable and reasonable use, however, no further reference to equitable and reasonable use or no significant harm are present'. While the 2013 Act may not have made explicit reference to the principles of IWL, it would have signified progression in the water sector. However, the 2013 Act has not been brought into effect, and as a result the Water Act of 1956 remains in force. Interestingly, despite the Act not being in force, some efforts have been made to implement some of the provisions of the Act: eight Basin Management Committees, as well as a Water Advisory Council, have been established and are in operation.[259]

As a means of compensating for the gap in the legal framework, several policy documents have been developed, including the Water Supply and Sanitation Policy of 2008[260] and the Integrated Water Resources Management Plan 2010. The Water Supply and Sanitation Policy links with Namibia's Vision 2030 and its NDP, stating that the financial performance of the water and sanitation sector will likely influence the pace of national development.[261] The Policy recognizes the link between the agricultural sector[262] and energy in relation to economic development.[263] However, more explicit references to sustainable development in the form of intergenerational equity or any mention of equitable and reasonable use or no significant harm are absent from the Policy.

Namibia's fifth NDP (NDP5) is the third five-year implementation plan to contribute to the achievement of Vision 2030.[264] Section 5.1 of NDP5 focuses on the need for increased investment in infrastructure development and looks at all aspects of the WEF nexus. In relation to water, it states that agriculture (irrigation) is the largest water consumer and will continue to be so until 2030. The focus within this section is on the use of resources for economic growth and industrialization, rather than for protection and preservation of resources. Overall, water scarcity is referenced as a problem throughout the document. It is stated that domestic purposes (including livestock) are given

259 ENSafrica & One World Group, *supra* note 228, at 190.

260 Government of Namibia, Water Supply and Sanitation Policy (July 2008), http://portal.unesco.org/fr/files/47370/12670872251Namibia_wsaspolicy.pdf/Namibia_wsaspolicy.pdf, accessed 20 July 2019.

261 *Id.*, s. 2.2.

262 *Id.*, s. 2.6.5.

263 *Id.*, s. 2.5.1.

264 Republic of Namibia, *National Plans: Vision 2030*, https://www.npc.gov.na/?page_id=210, accessed 20 July 2019.

priority in relation to water resources, with the second priority being economic activities such as mining, industry and irrigation.[265] The NDP makes no reference to the SDGs.

In its report regarding SDG indicator 6.5.2, Namibia notes that the main difficulty it faces in relation to implementing the ZAMCOM Agreement is with regard to flood management, the control of alien species and sustainable fishing.[266] The country highlights the projects undertaken by ZAMCOM and the commitment level of member states as a positive. Difficulties are also cited regarding data exchange, which often is described as being outdated and/or delayed. With regard to the main challenges the country faces in cooperating on transboundary waters, Namibia states the exchange of information and being a downstream user are difficult. When describing the main achievements, building trust and multi-country cooperation are highlighted.

Namibia, as with many of the other ZRB states, has a number of policy documents in place without the backing of a strong legal framework. The LNG approach could therefore be used in the revision of the legal framework to create a more streamlined approach to governance given the clear relevance of the WEF nexus and the SDGs to the existing development strategies of the country.

4.4.6 Tanzania

Tanzania's legal framework is relatively well developed, with the Water Resources Management Act (No. 11 of 2009) (WRMA) working in conjunction with the Environmental Management Act (No. 10 of 2004). Mention of equitable utilization is included in Article 98(1) of the WRMA, which states that 'the Minister may develop policies and strategies for the purposes of ensuring sustainable, equitable utilization and management of transboundary waters', however, this does not extend to any determination of what would be considered equitable use. Similarly, Tanzania does not explicitly provide for no significant harm to states within its water laws. However, it does provide in Article 59 of the 2005 Environmental Impact Assessment and Audit Regulations that where a project is likely to have transboundary impact, 'appropriate measures' are to be taken 'to mitigate any adverse impacts taking into account any existing treaties and agreements between the United Republic and the other States'. The WRMA has a specific chapter dedicated to transboundary

265 Namibian Water Supply and Sanitation Policy, *supra* note 260, at 36.

266 UNECE, 'Reporting under SDG Indicator 6.5.2: Namibia Country Report' (23 January 2018), https://www.unece.org/fileadmin/DAM/env/water/activities/Reporting_convention/All_countries/NAMIBIA_Reporting_SDG652_final_23.01.2018.pdf, accessed 3 February 2020.

resources.[267] It is largely empowering in nature, not requiring steps to be taken, but encouraging them. Such steps include actions such as collecting information about the environmental integrity of transboundary resources, developing policies which ensure equitable and sustainable use and measures to create a common database for transboundary waters. Section 100 of the WRMA also requires the minister to collect and analyse a list of minimum information in order to conduct transboundary functions, including the volume of water abstracted and beneficial uses, economic value, people dependant on the resources, information relating to discharges and environmental integrity. Section 32 also provides for the classification of water resources in relation to water equality objectives.

Tanzania also has developed policies and strategies in relation to the water sector, including the National Water Policy of 2002 and the National Water Sector Development Strategy 2006–2015. The National Water Policy includes the need to create a comprehensive framework for sustainable development, detailing a number of national targets. The policy also links to Tanzania's Vision 2025, which covers water resources management, and recognizes the WEF nexus linking to the national agricultural policy regarding rainfed agriculture and irrigation projects and to the energy sector, highlighting the importance of hydropower development. As with many of the Zambezi countries, the policy also states that an IWRM approach is adopted to ensure that 'multi-sectoral linkages' are included in the planning of water resource development.[268] In relation to transboundary waters, the Policy highlights the need for cooperation in accordance with the principle of equitable and reasonable use, as well as technical cooperation in research, data collection and information dissemination.[269] Tanzania's five-year NDP (2016/17–2020/21)[270] also makes various references to the importance of water, energy and food. Tanzania has also ratified both the SADC Revised Protocol and the ZAMCOM agreement.

Direct references to the SDGs are absent from the policy frameworks of Tanzania, and no report was submitted regarding indicator 6.5.2. However, from the information provided, it appears clear that utilizing an LNG approach could be useful for Tanzania in order to bring together the multiple plans,

267 United Republic of Tanzania, Water Resources Management Act (No. 11 of 2009), Part XII, http://extwprlegs1.fao.org/docs/pdf/tan96340.pdf, accessed 10 July 2019.

268 United Republic of Tanzania, *National Water Policy* (July 2002), http://www.tawasanet.or.tz/files/Tanzania%20water%20policy%20-%202002.pdf, accessed 10 July 2019, at 14.

269 *Id.*, at 16.

270 United Republic of Tanzania, *National Five Year Development Plan, 2016/17–2020/21* (June 2016), https://mof.go.tz/mofdocs/msemaji/Five%202016_17_2020_21.pdf, accessed 10 July 2019.

strategies and frameworks that have been put in place and can be supportively backed by the well-developed legal framework at a national level.

4.4.7 Zambia

Zambia's Water Resources Management Act (No. 21 of 2011) defines 'equitable' as 'fair, reasonable and just' in Article 2 and it ensures through Article 57 that 'the principles of equitable, reasonable and sustainable utilization of shared water resources' are operationalized by taking into account the factors of equitable and reasonable use as contained within Article 6 of the UNWC.[271] The Act demonstrates strong implementation of IWL principles, stating in Article 60(1)(c) that the use of water shall 'avoid or minimise the adverse impact of that use on other users of water'. However, this does not make the application to transboundary states explicit. A more explicit reference to transboundary resources is given in the 2011 Environmental Management Act, which states in Article 85(1) that 'the Minister may … collaborate with the relevant countries on environmental management programmes and measures to avoid and minimise transboundary environmental impacts'. Moreover, Article (2)(b) requires that the state of the environment report describe any significant adverse effects caused or likely to be caused and identify the causes and trends. Thus, the national legal regime on water governance in Zambia is fairly comprehensive and at a regional and basin level Zambia has also ratified both the SADC Revised Protocol and the ZAMCOM Agreement. However, the relationship between national goals and complying with international law is not always clear.

Zambia's Seventh National Development Plan (7NDP), for the period 2017–2021, contributes to its Vision 2030 and aims to work towards Zambia becoming a middle-income country by 2030.[272] In the context of agricultural development, the Plan notes 'increasing agricultural outputs leads to the development of both upstream and downstream activities, the consolidation of value chains and the expansion of agro-industries, which are significant sources of employment and present real opportunities for economic diversification'.[273] Therefore, while the 7NDP recognizes the relationship between agricultural activities on both upstream and downstream areas, it does not go further to discuss the relationship with water use. The Plan also states that 'irrigation development remains a key intervention for increasing crop diversification, production

271 Republic of Zambia, Water Resources Management Act (No. 21 of 2011).

272 Republic of Zambia, *Seventh National Development Plan* (*2017–2021*), http://extwprlegs1.fao.org/docs/pdf/zam170109.pdf, accessed 10 July 2019, at 7.

273 *Id.*, at 65.

and productivity'.[274] Regarding energy, the 7NDP states that there is need to increase supply in order to meet demand and, as a result, to 'promote investment in hydro, nuclear, geothermal, wind and solar energy generation'.[275] One of the development outcomes highlighted within the 7NDP is 'improved water resources development and management', because 'water resources infrastructure is a critical component in the provision of sustainable water resources management and services for engineered irrigation, drainage, water supply and sanitation, hydropower generation, flood control and food security'.[276] Therefore, the Plan explicitly recognizes the link between water resources and food security. The Plan cites strategies to address water development and management issues with a view to 'increasing availability of water resources for utilisation by productive sectors, for enhanced heath and sustainable economic growth'.[277] These strategies include the construction of small, medium and large dams to meet various water needs, 'particularly for domestic, agriculture and hydropower generation'.[278]

The SDGs are also referenced throughout the 7NDP, which stresses the importance of domesticating the goals within national plans.[279] In its report concerning indicator 6.5.2, Zambia noted inadequate capacity and resources as the main difficulty in implementing basin agreements.[280] Describing its main achievements, Zambia noted that a dedicated government department for international waters had been set up and that the key to success was ensuring that there is adequate funding to the sector and to work on building capacity for transboundary water resources management. With regard to data exchange, Zambia noted the inadequate collection by member states, although enhanced monitoring and management of water resources are the main benefits of data exchange. Zambia cited inadequate resources and the lack of a national mechanism for dealing with provisions of international waters instruments as challenges in cooperation on transboundary waters. The main achievements of transboundary cooperation were highlighted as data access and sharing, with the willingness to cooperate and support being key to the achievement of this.

274 *Id.*, at 66.

275 *Id.*, at 72.

276 *Id.*, at 78.

277 *Id.*, at 79.

278 *Id.*

279 See *Id.*

280 UNECE, 'Reporting under SDG Indicator 6.5.2: Zambia Country Report' (12 June 2017), https://www.unece.org/fileadmin/DAM/env/water/activities/Reporting_convention/All_countries/ZAMBIA_Reporting_SDG652_final_12.06.2017.pdf, accessed 10 May 2020.

The frameworks in place within Zambia are well developed and incorporate all aspects of the LNG approach. However, it is not clear how each of the developed strategies relates to one another and if there is any degree of mutual supportiveness. As with many of the other ZRB states, Zambia highlighted the difficulty of data exchange. The LNG approach could therefore be used to tie together existing frameworks, enhance mutual supportiveness and provide greater cooperation across sectors, which may contribute to increased information and data sharing.

4.4.8 Zimbabwe

Zimbabwe's Water Act (No. 21 of 1998) [Chapter 20:24] and the Environmental Management Agency Act 2002 (No. 13 of 2002) [Chapter 20:27] are the main pieces of legislation covering water resources, while the Zimbabwe National Water Authority Act (No. 11 of 1998) [Chapter 20:25] creates a statutory authority for implementation. The 2002 Environmental Management Agency Act, Article 99(c) and (d), states that the contents of an EIA report must 'give a detailed description of the likely impact the project may have on the environment or any segment thereof, covering the direct, indirect, cumulative, short-term and long-term effects of the project' and 'specify the measures proposed for eliminating, reducing or mitigating any anticipated adverse impacts'. A provision relating to significant harm, Article 99(e), states that an EIA report on a project shall 'indicate whether the environment of any other country is likely to be affected by the project and any measures to be taken to minimise any damage to that environment'.

A National Water Policy was published in 2012 in the context of collapsed water revenues and a decline in water supply infrastructure.[281] The Policy was designed around rebuilding the sector. As the Policy was developed after the legal framework, it is not represented in any legal provisions. Equitable and reasonable use is not present in the legal framework, however, it does provide for the promotion of equitable, efficient and sustainable allocation and distribution of resources nationally.[282] In addition, Section 7.6.5 of the National Water Policy states that the Policy 'promotes efficient and equitable utilisation of water resources', although this is not stated within the context of transboundary water resources. As previously noted, Zimbabwe has also signed the SADC Revised Protocol and has ratified the ZAMCOM Agreement.

281 Government of Zimbabwe, *National Water Policy* (August 2012), https://wsaz.files.wordpress.com/2019/02/zimbabwe-national-water-policy_2012.pdf, accessed 3 February 2020.

282 Government of Zimbabwe, 1998 Zimbabwe National Water Authority Act [Chapter 20:25], Art. 5(1)(d); 1998 Water Act [Chapter 20:24], Art. 6(1)(c).

Zimbabwe has also adopted *ad hoc* plans that do not have the same level of comprehensive development strategy as found in the NDPs of the other Zambezi riparian states. The most recent plans are the Medium-Term Plan (MTP, 2011–2015),[283] ZimAsset (2013–2018)[284] and the Ten-Point Plan (2015).[285] All of these documents are either approaching or have past their expiration date, as such it can be expected that new development strategies will be put in place imminently. The MTP discusses the importance of natural resources and cites sustainable development as a key principle of the plan. It further states that people have the right to benefit from environmental goods, but also have a duty to look after them.[286] Within the ZimAsset, references to the environment are less obvious, although reference is made to a number of environmental challenges, including water pollution. Emphasis is placed on water infrastructure and water supply related development.

In its report submitted with regard to indicator 6.5.2, Zimbabwe noted that integrated cooperation in water resources was key to the implementation of basin agreements.[287] In relation to the main issues with the operation of ZAMCOM, Zimbabwe noted limited financial resources towards country contributions and unexpected extreme events such as floods and droughts. The main achievement was highlighted as the coordination of water resources development. The main difficulties of data exchange were listed as the quality of data and harmonization across riparian states, with the main benefit being effective and informed water resources planning.

The frameworks in place in Zimbabwe provide little reference to key principles of IWL, the WEF nexus or the SDGs. However, the fact that the country reported on indicator 6.5.2 is positive and demonstrates its willingness to work towards the achievement of the SDGs. Once again, data exchange and harmonization were listed as difficulties within the ZRB. Thus, the LNG approach

283 Government of Zimbabwe, *Medium Term Plan 2011–2015* (Ministry of Economic Planning and Investment Promotion, 2011), http://www.zw.one.un.org/sites/default/files/Zimbabwe_MediumTermPlan2011-2015.pdf, accessed 3 February 2020.

284 Government of Zimbabwe, *Zimbabwe Agenda for Socio-Economic Transformation* (*Zim-Asset*) (October 2013–December 2018), http://www.zw.one.un.org/sites/default/files/Zim%20Asset.pdf, accessed 3 February 2020.

285 Gift Mugano, '10-point plan must inform the next blue print' *The Herald* (Zimbabwe, 22 July 2017) https://www.herald.co.zw/10-point-plan-must-inform-the-next-blue-print/, accessed 30 June 2020.

286 Government of Zimbabwe, Medium Term Plan, *supra* note 283.

287 UNECE, 'Reporting under SDG Indicator 6.5.2: Zimbabwe Country Report' (14 July 2017), https://www.unece.org/fileadmin/DAM/env/water/activities/Reporting_convention/All_countries/ZIMBABWE_Reporting_SDG652_final_14.07.2017.pdf, (accessed 10 May 2020).

could provide a means of channelling the drive to meet the SDGs towards the creation of an integrated approach for water governance.

4.5 *Takeaways from National Practice*

These practices of basin states provide strong evidence of most, if not all, components of the LNG approach to (shared) water governance. While there is an overall commitment to relevant principles and rules of IWL from basin states, some have made bold reference to the key principles and rules while others have not. Similarly, many basin states have relevant policies and a vision compatible with the WEF nexus and the SDGs, although priorities, emphasis, and the way in which they have been articulated varies from country to country. Within many countries a plethora of policies and legal frameworks exist, and difficulties with capacity are highlighted. It is possible that the adoption of an LNG approach could provide a framework for streamlining this multitude of frameworks, allowing capacity to be maximized. Of course, it must be noted that to alter existing frameworks requires capacity itself. Ideally, changes would also be adopted at a basin scale and subsequently implemented nationally in order to provide the best opportunity for harmonization. For this reason, the advocacy of the LNG approach is only demonstrated in the case of the ZRB as 'food for thought', and the authors provide this information with full awareness of the complexity and shortcomings in adopting the recommendations given.

5 Conclusion

This monograph sheds light on, firstly, the linkages between three conceptual frameworks—IWL, the WEF nexus and the SDGs, along with their strengths and shortcomings, in relation to the governance of international watercourses. It has detailed the differences between each of the frameworks and the opportunities that this may create with regard to the mitigation of trade-offs and the creation of synergies. IWL has been demonstrated as a permanent long-lasting normative framework of legal principles such as equitable and reasonable use and no significant harm. Yet, due to political will, capacity or vagueness of provisions, implementation of the normative standards offered by IWL is often a challenge. The WEF nexus, arguably the newest of the three frameworks (if the SDGs are viewed as an extension or a new 'phase' of the MDGs), can provide valuable insight into sectors beyond water, energy and food that are essential for holistic management of international watercourses. Its origin in industry brings a fresh perspective to the consideration of factors of equitable and reasonable use, as well as the possibility of aiding with the implementation of procedural provisions such as exchange of information.

The SDGs provide clear targets and indicators that can be linked to IWL and the WEF nexus, providing a tangible framework for governance and scope to maximize capacity by adopting an LNG approach. Although the SDGs are time-bound, set to expire in 2030, it is important to note that it is likely that the replacement framework will be in a similar vein, as has been the case in the progression from the MDGs to the SDGs. Therefore, although the framework is 'temporary' in nature, the goals and aspirations will continue, albeit with different format and focus; it is extremely likely that a subsequent global development agenda will be put in its place. We argue that even in the absence of a global development agenda, continental, regional and basin-level development and policy setting will continue; therefore, integrating water governance to development policy cannot be ignored in the years to come.

Notably, IWL provides predictability and stability as a legally binding normative framework,[288] while the WEF nexus and SDGs are conceptual and policy frameworks, respectively, that offer well-thought-out options and targets. That is not to say that one has more merit than another; the status of the WEF nexus and SDGs mean that states can easily adopt them at national or interstate levels, while becoming a part of an international legal framework can bring greater political difficulties. Equally, the IWL frameworks provide substantive and institutional mechanisms that are crucial to enforcing its principles, albeit with their own shortcomings, as discussed above. Nonetheless, it is important to recognize that an IWL framework, such as the UNWC (particularly given the status of its key principles as customary international law), is likely to have greater longevity than the WEF nexus or the SDG frameworks. Therefore, an integrated framework hinged on IWL provides a robust normative foundation upon which the more detailed, arguably more relatable, frameworks of the WEF nexus and SDGs can be implemented, allowing the whole framework to be firmly rooted upon foundational principles of water governance.

Thus, while each framework has distinct features and different advantages, this monograph finds that our understanding, interpretation and implementation of IWL could be enhanced and its gaps better remedied through the LNG integrated approach to the governance of shared watercourses. The substantive and procedural norms and commitments of IWL serve as the main pillar of this proposed approach, aided by (a) the WEF nexus, which enhances understanding regarding tension and trade-offs among the three key aspects of water use, and (b) the SDGs, which offer more focused and dynamic aspirations and concrete plans to the equitable and sustainable governance of water resources.

---

288 That is, legally binding upon those who have ratified a convention, although as stated above, many of the principles of the UNWC are recognized as customary international law.

This approach highlights the appropriateness of the WEF nexus and the SDG frameworks to implementing the principle of equitable and reasonable utilization, the duty to prevent significant harm and the duty to cooperate.

Secondly, after systematically applying the three frameworks to the ZRB at various levels, it is clear that IWL, the WEF nexus and the SDGs are well-recognized to varying extents across the ZRB. The WEF nexus is illustrated through the NDPs and development strategies of the ZRB states; principles of IWL are present within legal and policy frameworks; and while the SDGs specifically are not as widely found, notions of intergenerational equity and sustainable development more generally are common. Therefore, the ZRB should be recognized as a progressive example of an integrated approach to the governance of watercourses at regional, basin and national levels. This should be read with caution, however, given that there are a number of inconsistencies in the application of IWL, the WEF nexus and the SDGs at the national level which may challenge the realization of regional and basin-wide relevant laws, policies and programmes within each riparian state of the ZRB.

Thirdly, there continues to be a strong focus on IWRM within water sector strategies and legislation in the ZRB riparian states. The core elements of the LNG approach can therefore be found within some frameworks, however, linkages between each framework are weak. The implementation of new and old frameworks, including IWRM, and the LNGs as standalone agendas, will increase strain on capacity and financial resources, as well as likely decreasing efficiency and effectiveness. An integrated perspective, through the LNG approach detailed in this monograph could serve to maximise the benefits of the resources and as well as ensuring that each use is balanced and equitable. Further, by linking development strategies through an LNG approach, national governments can increase the temporal scope of their agenda, putting together a long-term strategy towards the successful implementation of international legal and policy frameworks. This approach can help them cooperate with each other with a better understanding of the potential benefits and risks of their plans and projects.

Fourthly, it has been shown that international (water) law is neither perfect nor does it exist in a vacuum. As stated by Fox and Sneddon, 'reliance on general principles of IWL, whose overarching goals support the maintenance of sovereign rights, undermine[s] ecological certainty'.[289] The authors continue:

289 C. A. Fox & C. Sneddon, *'Transboundary River Basin Agreements in the Mekong and Zambezi Basins: Enhancing Environmental Security or Securitizing the Environment?'*, 7, International Environmental Agreements: Politics, Law and Economics (2007) 237–261, 246.

> [R]epresenting basin ecosystems as simplified watercourses, where the flow of water in the main channel and major tributaries is virtually the only concern, discursively transforms them from unpredictable, variable, complex land-water ecosystems into legal structures and natural resources, both of which can be demarcated, reduced to parts, rationally managed, and subjected to substantive rules of law such as equitable and reasonable utilization.[290]

In essence, the authors argue that there are inherent problems in the notion of a river as a solely legal structure. The LNG approach advocated in this monograph could go some way to moving away from the state-based legal frameworks of IWL, towards a more holistic integrated approach that allows greater understanding to be given to the key principles of IWL based upon science, policy and aspirations of countries and communities. The fact that the WEF nexus is usually undertaken by scientists and impartial bodies independently of, or in collaboration with, concerned parties, suggests that it offers a much-needed contribution to implementing IWL and fosters cooperation from state officials or policy-makers.

In this regard, and as illustrated in the discussion above, the WEF nexus and SDG frameworks can help to fill the gap left by IWL, particularly in relation to the application of equitable and reasonable use and the factors which are used to determine it. The WEF nexus brings a unique viewpoint to the implementation of the legal framework, unpacking the key issues around water, energy and food, which are essential when taking into consideration the factors of Article 6 of the UNWC, such as social and economic need. The SDGs similarly provide specific objectives across all three sectors. Given that the SDGs are precise and measurable within a limited time frame, the normative framework benefits from this by making the implementation of the law more measurable. The WEF and the SDGs could also assist with the progression of IWL and provide a route through which future challenges such as population growth and climate change could be tackled. In particular, the SDGs are very dynamic in the sense that they succeeded the MDGs and are likely to be reviewed and replaced by other similar, if not identical, goals in the years to come. As a result, they are capable of making IWL instruments more progressive than they usually are, if they are appropriately and consensually integrated into the application of the law. It is likely that without taking into consideration additional soft law, policy or science-based frameworks, such as the WEF nexus and SDGs, IWL

290 *Id.*

could remain static; equally, without the strong normative framework of IWL underpinning their methodologies and monitoring processes, it is likely that the SDG targets will not be met and a comprehensive WEF nexus process will not be achieved.

To conclude, while being mindful of the risks of the proliferation of various water governance frameworks and the complexity of bringing them together, we submit that the LNG approach to transboundary water governance provides a strong case for a predictable, adaptable and measurable water governance framework, which adopts both a human and nature-centred approach capable of serving existing and future generations. Further, the LNG approach encourages international law scholarship to move from purely doctrinal to interdisciplinary research to support both better application and progressive development of the law and to mitigate real global and regional challenges of our time, including fierce competition over shared watercourses by states and communities. In this regard, the LNG approach to governing international watercourses may be among the key steps that the international community could consider to manage potential inter-state conflicts, promote development and cooperation, and tackle global issues such as climate change.

Acknowledgements

The authors would like to thank Stephanie Hawkins for her input to earlier drafts of this work, Jonathan Lautze and other reviewers of the Brill Perspective Series for their comments. This monograph is derived from research conducted under €5.5M four-year EU Horizon 2020 funded 'DAFNE' project which concerns the promotion of integrated and adaptive water resources management, explicitly addressing the WEF Nexus and aiming to promote a sustainable economy in regions where new infrastructure and expanding agriculture has to be balanced with social, economic and environmental needs. The project takes a multi- and interdisciplinary approach to the formation of a decision analytical framework (DAF) for participatory and integrated planning, to allow the evaluation of decisions based on social, economic and environmental needs, therefore reflective of sustainable development. The monograph therefore derives its perspectives from the interdisciplinarity within the project: thus, while retaining focus on legal frameworks at its core, the monograph will also look at policy frameworks and will take due note of the role to be played by other disciplines within water governance. For further information on the project see http://dafne-project.eu.

Bibliography

Aguilar, G., & I. Alejandro, *Governance of Shared Waters: Legal and Institutional Issues* (Gland: IUCN, 2011).

Alba, R., & A. Bolding, '*IWRM* Avant la Lettre*? Four Key Episodes in the Policy Articulation of IWRM in Downstream Mozambique*', 9, Water Alternatives (2016) 549–568.

Allan, A., & A. Rieu-Clarke, '*Good Governance and IWRM: A Legal Perspective*', 24, Irrigation and Drainage Systems (2010) 239–248.

Allouche, J., C. Middleton, & D. Gyawali, '*Technical Veil, Hidden Politics: Interrogating the Power Linkages behind the Nexus*', 8, Water Alternatives (2015) 610–626.

Bazilian, M., H. Rogner, M. Howells et al., '*Considering the Energy, Water and Food Nexus: Towards an Integrated Modelling Approach*', 39, Energy Policy (2011) 7896–7906.

Belinskij, A., '*Water-Energy-Food Nexus within the Framework of International Water Law*', 7:10, Water (Switzerland) (2015) 5396–5415.

Benson, D., A. K. Gain & J. J. Rouillard, '*Water Governance in a Comparative Perspective: From IWRM to a 'nexus' Approach?*', 8, Water Alternatives (2015) 756–773.

Bertule, M., P. Glennie, P. K. Bjørnsen et al., '*Monitoring Water Resources Governance Progress Globally: Experiences from Monitoring SDG Indicator 6.5.1 on Integrated Water Resources Management Implementation*', 10:12, Water (Switzerland) (2018) 1744.

Bhaduri, A., C. Ringler, I. Dombrowski et al., '*Sustainability in the Water—Energy—Food Nexus*', 40, Water International (2105) 723–732.

Boas, I., F. Biermann & N. Kanie, '*Cross-sectoral Strategies in Global Sustainability Governance: Towards a Nexus Approach*', 16, International Environmental Agreements: Politics, Law & Economics (2016) 449–464.

Boisson de Chazournes, L., M. M. Mbengue, M. Tignino et al., *The UN Convention on the Law of the Non-Navigational Uses of International Watercourses : A Commentary* (1st ed., Oxford: OUP, 2018).

Brunnée, J., & S. Toope, '*Environmental Security and Freshwater Resources: Ecosystem Regime Building*', 91, American Journal of International Law (1997) 26–59.

Brus, M. M. T., '*Soft Law in Public International Law: A Pragmatic or Principled Choice? Comparing the Sustainable Development Goals and the Paris Agreement*', in P. Westerman, J. Hage, S. Kirste & A. R. Mackor, (eds), *Legal Validity and Soft Law* (Cham: Springer, 2107), 243–266.

Burchi, S., '*The Future of Domestic Water Law: Trends and Developments Revisited, and Where Reform Is Headed*', 44, Water International (2019) 258–277.

Caflisch, L., '*Equitable and Reasonable Utilisation and Factors Relevant to Determining Such Utilisation (Articles 5 and 6)*' in L. Boisson de Chazournes, M. M. Mbengue, M. Tignino et al., *The UN Convention on the Law of the Non-Navigational Uses of International Watercourses : A Commentary* (1st ed., Oxford: OUP, 2018) 77–94.

Cai, X., Altchenko, Y., & Chavula, G., '*Availability and use of water resources*', in J. Lautze, Z. Phiri, V. Smakhtin & D. Saurchera (Eds.), *The Zambezi River Basin: Water and Sustainable Development* (Abingdon: Routledge, 2017) 7–28.

De Strasser, L., A. Lipponen, M. Howells et al., '*A Methodology to Assess the Water Energy Food Ecosystems Nexus in Transboundary River Basins*', 8:2, Water (Switzerland) (2016) 59.

Dellapenna, J. W., '*The Customary International Law of Transboundary Fresh Waters*', 1, International Journal of Global Environmental Issues (2001) 264–305.

Eckstein, G., R. K. Paisley, S. Burchi et al., *The Greening of Water Law: Managing Freshwater Resources for People and the Environment* (UNEP, 2010).

ENSAfrica & One World Group, *Equivalence Assessment of National Water Laws among Riparian States in the Zambezi River Basin: ZAMCOM Agreement Comparative Assessment & Gap Analysis* (11 September 2017).

Fader, M., C. Cranmer, R. Lawford & J. Engel-Cox, '*Toward an Understanding of Synergies and Trade-Offs Between Water, Energy, and Food SDG Targets*', 6, Frontiers in Environmental Science (2018) 112. DOI:10.3389/fenvs.2018.00112.

Food and Agriculture Organization of the United Nations (FAO), '*The Zambezi Basin*', in *Irrigation Potential in Africa: A Basin Approach*, FAO Land and Water Bulletin 4 (Rome: FAO, 1997).

Fox, C. A., & C. Sneddon, '*Transboundary River Basin Agreements in the Mekong and Zambezi Basins: Enhancing Environmental Security or Securitizing the Environment?*', 7, International Environmental Agreements: Politics, Law and Economics (2007) 237–261.

Fuentes, X., '*The Criteria for the Equitable Utilization of International Rivers*', 67:1, The British Yearbook of International Law (1997) 337–412.

Grey, D., & C. Sadoff, '*Beyond the River: The Benefits of Cooperation on International Rivers*', 47, Water Science and Technology (2003) 91–96.

Hoff, H., *Understanding the Nexus. Background Paper for the Bonn 2011 Conference: The Water, Energy and Food Security Nexus* (Stockholm: Stockholm Environment Institute, 2011).

Honkonen, T., '*Water Security and Climate Change: The Need for Adaptive Governance*', 20, Potchefstroom Electronic Law Journal (2017).

Human Rights Council, 'Human rights and access to safe drinking water and sanitation', UN Doc A/HRC/Res/15/9 (6 October 2010).

International Law Commission, '*Draft Articles on the Law of the Non-navigational Uses of International Watercourses and Commentaries Thereto and Resolution on Transboundary Confined Groundwater*', in *Report of the ILC on the Work of its Forty-sixth Session (2 May–22 July 1994)*, UN Doc. A/49/10.

International Law Commission, '*Draft Articles on Prevention of Transboundary Harm from Hazardous Activities, with commentaries*' (11 May 2001), in *Report of the*

International Law Commission on the Work of its Fifty-third Session 23 April–1 June and 2 July–10 August 2001, UN Doc A/56/10.

Lankford, B., '*Does Article 6 (Factors Relevant to Equitable and Reasonable Utilization) in the UN Watercourses Convention Misdirect Riparian Countries?*', 38, Water International (2013) 130–145.

Leb, C., *Cooperation in the Law of Transboundary Water Resources* (Cambridge: Cambridge University Press, 2013).

Leb, C., '*One Step at a Time: International Law and the Duty to Cooperate in the Management of Shared Water Resources*', 40, Water International (2014) 21–32.

Leb, C., '*General Obligation to Cooperate and Regular Exchange of Data and Information (Articles 8 and 9)*', in L. Boisson de Chazournes, M. M. Mbengue, M. Tignino, K. Sangbana & J. Rudall (eds.), *The UN Convention on the Law of the Non-Navigational Uses of International Watercourses: A Commentary* (1st ed., Oxford: OUP, 2018) 123–140.

Leb, C., '*Data Innovations for Transboundary Freshwater Resources Management: Are Obligations Related to Information Exchange Still Needed?*', 4.4, Brill Research Perspectives in International Water Law (2020).

Lim, M., '*Is Water Different from Biodiversity? Governance Criteria for the Effective Management of Transboundary Resources*', 23:1, Review of European, Comparative and International Environmental Law (2014) 96–110.

Lowe, V., '*Sustainable Development and Unsustainable Arguments*', in A. Boyle & D. Freestone (Eds.), *International Law and Sustainable Development: Past Achievements and Future Challenges* (Oxford: OUP, 1999) 19–37.

McCaffrey, S. C., *The Law of International Watercourses* (2nd ed., Oxford: OUP, 2007).

McCaffrey, S. C., '*The Path to the UN Watercourses Convention and Beyond*', in L. Boisson de Chazournes, M. M. Mbengue, M. Tignino, K. Sangbana & J. Rudall (eds.), *The UN Convention on the Law of the Non-Navigational Uses of International Watercourses: A Commentary* (1st ed., Oxford: OUP, 2018) 1–18.

McCaffrey, S. C., '*The Customary Law of International Watercourses*', in M. Tignino & C. Bréthaut (Eds.), *Research Handbook on Freshwater Law and International Relations* (Cheltenham: Edward Elgar, 2018) 147–174.

McCaffrey, S., '*Introductory Remarks: The Last Drop: Practical Tools for Addressing Transboundary Water Crises*', in *Proceedings of the 113th ASIL Annual Meeting* (Cambridge: Cambridge University Press, 2019) 313–329.

McCaffrey, S. C., C. Leb & R. Denoon, '*Introduction to the Research Handbook on International Water Law*', in S. C. McCaffrey, C. Leb & R. T. Denoon (Eds.), *Research Handbook on International Water Law* (Cheltenham: Edward Elgar, 2019) 1–9.

McIntyre, O., '*The Role of Customary Rules and Principles of International Environmental Law in the Protection of Shared International Freshwater Resources*', 46, Natural Resources Journal (2006) 157–210.

McIntyre, O., *Environmental Protection of International Watercourses under International Law* (Aldershot: Ashgate Publishing, 2007).

McIntyre, O., '*The Protection of Freshwater Ecosystems Revisited: Towards a Common Understanding of the "Ecosystems Approach" to the Protection of Transboundary Water Resources*', 23, Review of European, Comparative and International Environmental Law (2014) 88–95.

McIntyre, O., '*Substantive Rules of International Water Law*', in A. Rieu-Clarke, A. Allan & S. Hendry (Eds.), *Routledge Handbook of Water Law and Policy* (London and New York: Routledge, 2017) 234–246.

McIntyre, O., '*International Water Law and SDG 6: Mutually Reinforcing Paradigms*', in D. French & L. J. Kotzé (Eds.), *Sustainable Development Goals : Law, Theory and Implementation* (Cheltenham: Edward Elgar, 2018) 173–200.

McIntyre, O., '*Environmental Protection and the Ecosystem Approach*', in S. C. McCaffrey, C. Leb & R. T. Denoon (Eds.), *Research Handbook on International Water Law* (Cheltenham: Edward Elgar 2019) 126–146.

Middleton, C., J. Allouche, D. Gyawali & S. Allen, '*The Rise and Implications of the Water-Energy-Food Nexus in Southeast Asia through an Environmental Justice Lens*', 8:1, Water Alternatives (2015) 627–654.

Molle, F., '*Nirvana Concepts, Narratives and Policy Models: Insight from the Water Sector*', 1:1, Water Alternatives (2008) 131–156.

Moynihan, R., '*Inland Water Biodiversity: International Law on Protection of Transboundary Freshwater Ecosystems and Biodiversity*', in M. G. Faure (Ed.), *Elgar Encyclopedia of Environmental Law* (Cheltenham: Edward Elgar, 2016) 189–202.

Mugano, G., '10-point plan must inform the next blue print' *The Herald* (Zimbabwe, 22 July 2017).

Muller, M., '*The "Nexus" as a Step Back towards a More Coherent Water Resource Management Paradigm*', 8:1, Water Alternatives (2015) 675–694.

Nhamo, L., B. Ndlela, C. Nhemachena et al., '*The Water-Energy-Food Nexus: Climate Risks and Opportunities in Southern Africa*', 10:5, Water (Switzerland) (2018) 567.

Nilsson, M., D. Griggs & M. Visbeck, '*Policy: Map the Interactions between Sustainable Development Goals*', 534, Nature (2016) 320–322.

Okowa, P., '*Procedural Obligations in International Environmental Agreements*', 67:1, British Yearbook of International Law (1996) 275–336.

Onencan, A. M., & B. V. Van de Walle, '*Equitable and Reasonable Utilization: Reconstructing the Nile Basin Water Allocation Dialogue*', 10:6, Water (Switzerland) (2018) 707.

Orme, M., Z. Cuthbert, F. Sindico et al., '*Good Transboundary Water Governance in the 2015 Sustainable Development Goals: A Legal Perspective*', 40:7, Water International (2015) 969–983.

Oyebande, L., & S. Odunuga, '*Climate Change Impact on Water Resources at the Transboundary Level in West Africa: The Cases of the Senegal, Niger and Volta Basins*', 4, The Open Hydrology Journal (2010) 163–172.

Pahl-Wostl, C., A. Bhaduri & A. Bruns, '*Editorial Special Issue: The Nexus of Water, Energy and Food—An Environmental Governance Perspective*', 90, Environmental Science & Policy (2018) 161–163.

Pahl-Wostl, C., '*Governance of the Water-Energy-Food Security Nexus: A Multi-Level Coordination Challenge*', 92, Environmental Science & Policy (2019) 356–367.

Reinhard, S., J. Verhagen, W. Wolters & R. Ruben, *Water-Food-Energy-Nexus: A Quick Scan* (Wageningen: Wageningen Economic Research, 2017).

Rieu-Clarke, A., & R. Kinna, '*Can Two Global UN Water Conventions Effectively Co-exist? Making the Case for a 'Package Approach' to Support Institutional Coordination*', 23:1, Review of European, Comparative & International Environmental Law (2014) 15–31.

Rieu-Clarke, A., A. Allan & S. Hendry (Eds.), *Routledge Handbook of Water Law and Policy* (London and New York: Routledge, 2017).

Rieu-Clarke, A., '*Definition and Use of Terms*', in L. Boisson de Chazournes, M. M. Mbengue, M. Tignino et al., *The UN Convention on the Law of the Non-Navigational Uses of International Watercourses : A Commentary* (1st ed., Oxford: OUP, 2018) 45–50.

Salman, S. M. A., '*Legal Regime for Use and Protection of International Watercourses in Southern African Region: Evolution and Context*', 41, Natural Resources Journal (2001) 981–1022.

Salman, S. M. A., '*The United Nations Watercourses Convention Ten Years Later: Why Has Its Entry into Force Proven Difficult?*', 32:1, Water International (2007) 1–15.

Salman, S. M. A., '*The Obligation not to Cause Significant Harm (Article 7)*', in L. Boisson de Chazournes, M. M. Mbengue, M. Tignino et al., *The UN Convention on the Law of the Non-Navigational Uses of International Watercourses : A Commentary* (1st ed., Oxford: OUP, 2018) 95–122.

Saruchera, D., J. Lautze, J. Mwale et al., '*Transboundary Water Cooperation: Taking Stock and Looking Forward*', in J. Lautze, Z. Phiri, V. Smakhtin & D. Saurchera (Eds.), *The Zambezi River Basin: Water and Sustainable Development* (Abingdon: Routledge, 2017) 175–192.

Schmeier, S., A. K. Gerlak & S. Blumstein, '*Clearing the Muddy Waters of Shared Watercourses Governance: Conceptualizing International River Basin Organizations*', 16, International Environmental Agreements: Politics, Law and Economics (2106) 597–619.

Schweizer, R., & C. Bréthaut, '*From the Promises of International Water Management Trends to the Reality of Policies and Practices: Some Conclusive Thoughts*', in C. Bréthaut & R. Schweizer (Eds.), *A Critical Approach to International Water*

Management Trends: Policy and Practice (London: Palgrave Macmillan, 2018) 269–293.

Simpson, G. B., & G. P. W. Jewitt, '*The Development of the Water-Energy-Food Nexus as a Framework for Achieving Resource Security: A Review*', 7, Frontiers in Environmental Science (2019). DOI:10.3389/fenvs.2019.00008.

Smajgl, A., J. Ward & L. Pluschke, '*The Water-Food-Energy Nexus—Realising a New Paradigm*', 533, Journal of Hydrology (2016) 533–540.

Soils Incorporated (Pvt) Ltd and Chalo Environmental and Sustainable Development Consultants, *Kariba Dam Case Study: Zambia and Zimbabwe Final Report*, prepared for the World Commission on Dams, Cape Town (2000).

Spijkers, O., '*The Cross-fertilization between the Sustainable Development Goals and International Water Law*', 25:1, Review of European Comparative & International Environmental Law (2016) 39–49.

Spijkers, O., '*Intergenerational Equity and the Sustainable Development Goals*', 10:11, Sustainability (2018) 3836.

Stephan, R. M., R. H. Mohtar, B. Daher et al., '*Water—Energy—Food Nexus: A Platform for Implementing the Sustainable Development Goals*', 43:3, Water International (2018) 472–479.

Subramanian, A., B. Brown & A. Wolf, '*Understanding and Overcoming Risks to Cooperation along Transboundary Rivers*', 16, Water Policy (2014) 824–843.

Swain, A., '*Politics or Development: Sharing of International Rivers in the South*', in J. Öjendal, S. Hansson & S. Hellberg (Eds.), *Politics and Development in a Transboundary Watershed: The Case of the Lower Mekong Basin* (Dordrecht: Springer, 2012) 19–35.

Tanzi, A., *The Consolidation of International Water Law: A Comparative Analysis of the UN and UNECE Water Conventions* (Editoriale Scientifica Napoli, 2017).

Tarlock, A. D., '*Safeguarding International River Ecosystems in Times of Scarcity*', 3, University of Denver Water Law Journal (2000) 231–272.

Terrapon-Pfaff, J., W. Ortiz, C. Dienst & M-C. Gröne, '*Energising the WEF Nexus to Enhance Sustainable Development at Local Level*', 223, Journal of Environmental Management (2018) 409–416.

The World Bank, *The Zambezi River Basin: A Multi-Sector Investment Opportunities Analysis, Volume 4: Summary Report* (Washington, DC: The World Bank, 2010).

Tignino, M., & C. Bréthaut (Eds.), *Research Handbook on Freshwater Law and International Relations* (Cheltenham: Edward Elgar, 2018).

Tilmant, A., W. Kinzelbach, D. Juizo et al., '*Economic Valuation of Benefits and Costs Associated with the Coordinated Development and Management of the Zambezi River Basin*', 14, Water Policy (2012) 490–508.

Tilmant, A., '*Hydropower and the Water-Energy-Food Nexus*', in J. Lautze, Z. Phiri, V. Smakhtin & D. Saurchera (Eds.), *The Zambezi River Basin: Water and Sustainable Development* (Abingdon: Routledge, 2017) 82–101.

Tumbare, M. J., 'The Zambezi River: Its Threats and Opportunities', presented at The Zambezi River: It's Threats and Opportunities, 7th River Symposium, 1–3 September 2004, Brisbane, Australia.

UN Committee on Economic, Social and Cultural Rights, '*General Comment No.15: The Right to Water (Arts. 11 and 12 of the Covenant)*', UN Doc. E/C.12/2002/11 (20 January 2003).

UN General Assembly, '*Transforming Our World: The 2030 Agenda for Sustainable Development*', 21 October 2015, UNGA Resolution 70/1, UN Doc. A/RES/70/1.

UN General Assembly, *Official Records*, 99th Plenary Meeting, 21 May 1997, UN Doc. A/51/PV.99.

UN General Assembly, '*The Human Right to Water and Sanitation*', 28 July 2010, UNGA Resolution 64/292, UN Doc. A/RES/64/292.

UN General Assembly, '*United Nations Millennium Declaration*', 18 September 2000, UNGA Resolution 55/2, UN Doc A/RES/55/2.

UN-Water, *Water Security & the Global Water Agenda: A UN-Water Analytical Brief* (Hamilton, ON: United Nations University, 2013).

UN-Water, *Water and Sanitation Interlinkages across the 2030 Agenda for Sustainable Development* (Geneva: UN-Water, 2016).

UN-Water, *Integrated Monitoring Guide for Sustainable Development Goal 6 on Water and Sanitation: Targets and Global Indicators* (Geneva: UN-Water, 14 July 2017).

UNECE (United Nations Economic Commission for Europe), *Guide to Implementing the Water Convention* (New York and Geneva: United Nations, 2013).

UNECE, *Reconciling Resource Uses in Transboundary Basins: Assessment of the Water-Food-Energy-Ecosystems Nexus* (New York and Geneva: United Nations, 2015).

UNECE, *Methodology for Assessing the Water-Food-Energy-Ecosystems Nexus in Transboundary Basins and Experiences from its Application: Synthesis* (New York and Geneva: United Nations, 2018).

United Nations, *Agenda 21: A Programme for Action for Sustainable Development*, UN Doc A/CONF.151/26 (Vol. II) (13 June 1992), Annex II.

United Nations, '*Declaration of the United Nations Conference on the Human Environment*', *in Report of the United Nations Conference on the Human Environment, Stockholm, 5–16 June 1972*, UN Doc A/CONF.48/14/REV.1 (New York: United Nations, 1973).

United Nations General Assembly, '*Rio Declaration on Environment and Development, Rio de Janeiro, 13 June 1992*', in *Report of the United Nations Conference on Environment and Development*, UN Doc. A/CONF.151/26 (12 August 1992), Annex 1.

United Nations Development Programme (UNDP), *Human Development Report 2016: Human Development for Everyone* (New York: UNDP, 2016).

United Nations World Water Assessment Programme (WWAP), *The United Nations World Water Development Report 2017: Wastewater, The Untapped Resource* (Paris: UNESCO, 2017).

United Nations and UNESCO (on behalf of UN-Water), *Progress on Transboundary Water Cooperation: Global Baseline for SDG Indicator 6.5.2* (Paris: UNESCO, 2018).

Van Der Zaag, P., I. M. Seyam & H. H. G. Savenije, '*Towards Measurable Criteria for the Equitable Sharing of International Water Resources*', 4:1, Water Policy (2002) 19–32.

Van der Zaag, P., '*Asymmetry and Equity in Water Resources Management Critical Institutional Issues for Southern Africa*', 21:12, Water Resources Management (2007) 1993–2004.

Waughray, D. (Ed.), *Water Security: The Water-Food-Energy-Climate Nexus: The World Economic Forum Water Initiative* (Washington, DC: Island Press, 2011).

Wegerich, K., & O. Olsson, '*Late Developers and the Inequity of "Equitable Utilization" and the Harm of "Do No Harm"*', 35:6, Water International (2010) 707–717.

Wichelns, D., '*The Water-Energy-Food Nexus: Is the Increasing Attention Warranted, from Either a Research or Policy Perspective?*', 69, Environmental Science and Policy (2017) 113–123.

World Water Council, '*Messages and Policy Recommendations*', Budapest Water Summit, 28–30 November 2016 (Budapest: Ministry of Foreign Affairs and Trade of Hungary, 2016).

Wouters, P. K., '*An Assessment of Recent Developments in International Watercourse Law through the Prism of the Substantive Rules Governing Use Allocation (River Basins)*', 36:2, Natural Resources Journal (1996) 417–439.

Wouters, P., S. Vinogradov, A. Allan et al., *Sharing Transboundary Waters: An Integrated Assessment of Equitable Entitlement: The Legal Assessment Model*, IHP-VI, Technical Documents in Hydrology No.74 (Paris: UNESCO, 2005).

Yihdego, Z., & A. Rieu-Clarke, '*An Exploration of Fairness in International Law through the Blue Nile and GERD*', 41:4, Water International (2016) 528–549.

Yihdego, Z., '*The Fairness "Dilemma" in Sharing the Nile Waters: What Lessons from the Grand Ethiopian Renaissance Dam for International Law?*', 2:2, Brill Research Perspectives in International Water Law (2017).

Zambezi Watercourse Commission, *Integrated Water Resources Management Strategy and Implementation Plan for the Zambezi River Basin: At a Glance* (Harare: ZAMCOM, 2016).

Zeitoun, M., N. Mirumachi & J. Warner, '*Transboundary Water Interaction II: The Influence of "Soft" Power*', 11, International Environmental Agreements: Politics, Law and Economics (2011) 159–178.

Zeitoun, M., '*The Relevance of International Water Law to Later-developing Upstream States*', 40:7, Water International (2015) 949–968.

Legislation

Agreement between the Government of the Republic of Angola and The Government of the Republic of Namibia on the Establishment of Cuvelai Watercourse Commission (CUVECOM), 16 September 2014.
Agreement between the Republic of Zimbabwe and the Republic of Zambia concerning the utilization of the Zambezi River (signed at Harare, 28 July 1987).
Agreement on the Establishment of the Zambezi Watercourse Commission (ZAMCOM) (signed 13 August 2004, in force June 19 2011).
Charter of Waters of Senegal River (Charte des Eaux du Fleuve Sénégal) signed May 28th 2002.
Convention on the Law of the Non-Navigational Uses of International Watercourses (adopted 21 May 1997, in force 17 August 2014) UN Doc A/51/869.
Convention on the Protection and Use of Transboundary Watercourses and International Lakes (adopted 17 March 1992, in force 6 October 1996) 1936 UNTS 269.
Dar-es-Salaam Declaration on Agriculture and Food Security in the SADC Region (15 May 2004).
International Covenant on Economic Social and Cultural Rights (ICESCR) (adopted 16 December 1966, in force 3 January 1976).
Protocol on Energy, Southern African Development Community (adopted 24 August 1996, in force 17 April 1998).
Revised Protocol on Shared Watercourses in the Southern African Development Community (adopted 7 August 2000, in force 22 September 2003).

Angola

1998 Environmental Law No. 5/98.
Law on Water Use (No 6 of 2002), 21st June 2002 (Lei n 6/02).

Botswana

Borehole Act 1956 [Chapter 34:02].
Draft Water Bill 2005, available at http://www.orangesenqurak.org/UserFiles/File/National%20Water%20Departments/Botswana/draft%20Botswana%20WATER_BILL%201.pdf. last accessed 10 July 2019.
Environmental Assessment Act (No.10 of 2011).
Water Act of 1969 [Chapter 34:01].
Water Utilities Corporation Act 1970 [Chapter 74:02].
Water Works Act 1969 [Chapter 34:03].

Malawi

2013 Water Management Act (No. 2 of 2013), available at <http://extwprlegs1.fao.org/docs/pdf/mlw167598.pdf> last accessed 10 August 2019.

2001 Irrigation Act (No. 16 of 2001).

Mozambique

1997 Act No. 20/97.

1991 Act No. 16/91.

Namibia

1956 Water Act (54 of 1956).

2004 Water Resources Management Act (24 of 2004).

2013 Water Resources Management Act (No. 11 of 2013).

2007 Environmental Management Act (No. 7 of 2007).

Tanzania

2009 Water Resources Management Act (No. 11 of 2009) available at http://extwprlegs1.fao.org/docs/pdf/tan96340.pdf (last accessed 10 July 2019).

2004 Environmental Management Act (10 of 2004).

2005 Environmental Impact Assessment and Audit Regulations, (G.N. No. 349 of 2005).

Zambia

2011 Water Resources Management Act (No. 21 of 2011).

2011 Environmental Management Act (No. 12 of 2011).

Zimbabwe

2002 Environmental Management Agency Act [Chapter 20:27].

1998 Zimbabwe National Water Authority Act [Chapter 20:25].

1998 Water Act [Chapter 20:24].

Policy

Department of Water Affairs, Ministry of Minerals, Energy and Water Resources, *Botswana Integrated Water Resources Management & Water Efficiency Plan* (L. Kikobe, Ed.) (Gaborone: Government of Botswana, 2013), https://www.gwp.org/globalassets/global/activities/impact-stories/further-reading/iwrm-we-plan.pdf, accessed 10 July 2019.

Government of Botswana, *National Water Policy* (October 2012), http://extwprlegs1.fao.org/docs/pdf/bot179129.pdf, accessed 10 July 2019.

Government of Botswana, *National Development Plan 11, Volume 1, April 2017–March 2023*, http://extwprlegs1.fao.org/docs/pdf/bot175398.pdf, accessed 10 May 2020.

Government of Malawi, *National Water Resources Master Plan* (2013), https://openjicareport.jica.go.jp/pdf/12184537_07.pdf, accessed 12 April 2020.

Government of Malawi, *National Water Policy* (2005), https://cepa.rmportal.net/Library/government-publications/National%20Water%20Policy%202005.pdf/at_download/file, accessed 20 August 2019.

Government of Malawi, *The Malawi Growth and Development Strategy (MGDS) III (2017–2022)* (November 2017), https://www.undp.org/content/dam/malawi/docs/UNDP_Malawi_MGDS)%20III.pdf, accessed 20 August 2019.

Government of Malawi, *Vision 2020: The National Long-term Development Perspective for Malawi: A Summary* (Lilongwe: National Economic Council 2000), https://cepa.rmportal.net/Library/government-publications/Vision%202020-%20The%20National%20Long%20Term%20Development%20Perspective%20for%20Malawi.pdf/at_download/file, accessed 10 May 2020.

Government of Mozambique, *Agenda 2025*, https://www.foresightfordevelopment.org/sobipro/55/130-agenda-2025-the-nations-vision-and-strategies, accessed 10 August 2019.

Government of Namibia, *Water Supply and Sanitation Policy* (July 2008), http://portal.unesco.org/fr/files/47370/12670872251Namibia_wsaspolicy.pdf/Namibia_wsaspolicy.pdf, accessed 20 July 2019.

Government of Namibia, *5th National Development Plan (2017/18–2021/22)*, http://www.gov.na/documents/10181/14226/NDP+5/, accessed 11 May 2020.

Republic of Namibia, *National Plans: Vision 2030*, https://www.npc.gov.na/?page_id=210, accessed 20 July 2019.

United Republic of Tanzania, *National Water Policy* (July 2002), http://www.tawasanet.or.tz/files/Tanzania%20water%20policy%20-%202002.pdf, accessed 10 July 2019.

Government of the United Republic of Tanzania, *National Water Sector Development Strategy (2006–2015)*, http://extwprlegs1.fao.org/docs/pdf/tan169532.pdf, accessed 10 July 2019.

Government of the United Republic of Tanzania, *National Five Year Development Plan, 2016/17–2020/21* (June 2016), https://mof.go.tz/mofdocs/msemaji/Five%202016_17_2020_21.pdf, accessed 10 July 2019.

Government of the United Republic of Tanzania, *Vision 2025*, https://mof.go.tz/mofdocs/overarch/vision2025.htm, accessed 10 August 2019.

Government of Zambia, *Seventh National Development Plan (20172021)*, http://extwprlegs1.fao.org/docs/pdf/zam170109.pdf, accessed 10 July 2019.

Government of Zambia, *Vision 2030*, https://www.mndp.gov.zm/?wpfb_dl=89, accessed 11 May 2020.

Government of Zimbabwe, *National Water Policy* (August 2012), https://wsaz.files.wordpress.com/2019/02/zimbabwe-national-water-policy_2012.pdf, last accessed 3 February 2020.

Government of Zimbabwe, *Medium Term Plan (2011–2015)*, http://extwprlegs1.fao.org/docs/pdf/zim151067.pdf, accessed 3 February 2020.

Government of Zimbabwe, *Agenda for Socio-Economic Transformation (Zim-Asset), October 2013–December 2018*, http://www.zw.one.un.org/sites/default/files/Zim%20Asset.pdf, accessed 3 February 2020.

SADC, Draft WEF Nexus Operational Framework Reviewed at Transboundary River Basin Level' The Water, Energy & Food Security Resource Platform, https://www.water-energy-food.org/resources/resources-detail/implementation-sadc-s-draft-wef-nexus-operational-framework-reviewed-at-transboundary-river-basin-level/, accessed 27 May 2019.

SADC, Regional Agricultural Policy (August 2014), https://www.nepad.org/publication/sadc-regional-agricultural-policy-0, accessed 20 April 2019.

SADC, Regional Energy Access Strategy and Action Plan (March 2010), http://www.euei-pdf.org/en/sadc-regional-energy-access-strategy-and-action-plan, accessed 20 April 2019.

SADC, Regional Water Policy (August 2005), https://www.sadc.int/files/1913/5292/8376/Regional_Water_Policy.pdf, accessed 15 June 2019.

SADC, Regional Water Strategy (adopted June 2006), https://www.sadc.int/files/2513/5293/3539/Regional_Water_Strategy.pdf, accessed 15 June 2019.

SADC, Regional Infrastructure Development Master Plan (adopted August 2012), https://www.sadc.int/files/7513/5293/3530/Regional_Infrastructure_Development_Master_Plan_Executive_Summary.pdf, accessed 15 June 2019.

SADC, Regional Strategic Action Plan on Integrated Water Resources Development and Management, Phase IV (2016–2020), https://www.sadc.int/files/9914/6823/9107/SADC_Water_4th_Regional_Strategic_Action_Plan_English_version.pdf, accessed 15 June 2019.

ZAMCOM, Rules and Procedures for Sharing of Data and Information Related to the Management and Development of the Zambezi Watercourse (adopted 25 February 2016, effective 26 March 2016), http://www.zambezicommission.org/sites/default/files/clusters_pdfs/16.07.28-Rules_ProceduresForDataSharing_Adopted-by-Council_FinalEditing_Ver10_FINAL.pdf, accessed 10 September 2019.

ZAMCOM, Integrated Water Resources Management Strategy and the Implementation Plan for the Zambezi River Basin (April 2008), http://www.zambezicommission.org/sites/default/files/clusters_pdfs/Zambezi%20River_Basin_IWRM_Strategy_ZAMSTRAT.pdf, accessed 9 June 2019.

Case Law

Colorado v. New Mexico (1982) 459 US 176.

Case Concerning the Continental Shelf between Tunisia and Libyan Arab Jamahiriya (Tunisia/Libyan Arab Jamahiriya), Judgment, [1982] ICJ Rep 18.

Case Concerning Maritime Delimitation in the Area between Greenland and Jan Mayen (Denmark v. Norway), Judgment, [1993] ICJ Rep 38.

Corfu Channel Case (United Kingdom/Albania), Judgment (Merits), [1949] ICJ Rep 4.

Delimitation of the Maritime Boundary in the Gulf of Maine Area (Canada v. United States), Judgment, [1984] ICJ Rep 165.

Gabčíkovo-Nagymoros Project (Hungary v. Slovakia), Judgment (Merits), [1997] ICJ Rep 4.

Government of India, *Report of the Narmada Water Disputes Tribunal* (New Delhi, 1979), Vol I.

Government of India, *Report of the Krishna Water Disputes Tribunal* (New Delhi, 1973), Vol. II.

North Sea Continental Shelf Cases (Federal Republic of Germany/Denmark; Federal Republic of Germany/Netherlands), Judgment (Merits), [1969] ICJ Rep 3.

Pulp Mills on the River Uruguay (Argentina v. Uruguay), Judgment, [2010] ICJ Rep 14.

Territorial Jurisdiction of the International Commission of the River Oder, [1929] Judgement No. 16, P.C.I.J., Series A, No. 23.

Trail Smelter Arbitration (United States v. Canada), 3 R.I.A.A. 1911 [1938, 1941].

www.ingramcontent.com/pod-product-compliance
Lightning Source LLC
Chambersburg PA
CBHW031331230926
51848CB00001B/178